Strategic
Perspectives
from Hospitality
Leaders

旅游酒店业引领者之高端视角

（澳）金博蓝 张玉艳 黄志恩◎主编

Brian King Catherine Cheung Alan Wong Chief Editors

中国旅游出版社

Interviewee Biographies 受访者简历

陈雪明　Chen Xueming

陈雪明，著名连锁酒店品牌运营专家，金陵酒店管理公司董事、总裁。

Mr. Chen Xueming is an expert in hotel management and brand operation for famous chain hotels. He is also President of Nanjing Tourism Hotel Association, and Vice President of Hotel Investors Branch.

金杜　Jin Du

金杜，知名品牌民宿宛若故里的创始人。

Ms. Jin Du is the founder of the well-known brand Home Away from Home Resort（宛若故里）.

魏黎　Philip Wei

魏黎，邦泰峡国际酒店集团创始人。

Mr. Philip Wei is the founder of BTL Hospitality of China.

郭敬文　Clement Kwok

郭敬文，拥有法国荣誉军团骑士团勋章，于 2002 年 2 月担任香港上海大酒店有限公司董事总经理及行政总裁。

Mr. Clement Kwok, Knight of the Legion of Honour, was appointed Managing Director & Chief Executive Officer of the Hongkong and Shanghai Hotels, Limited (HSH) in February 2002.

郑志雯 Sonia Cheng

郑志雯带领一个经验丰富的行业领导者团队，将瑰丽酒店集团打造成为全球发展最快的国际酒店公司之一，在北美、欧洲、中东和亚洲开设有 60 多家酒店。

Ms. Sonia Cheng leads a team of seasoned industry leaders to establish Rosewood Hotel Group as one of the fastest growing international hotel companies in the world with over 60 hotels across North America, Europe, Middle East and Asia.

田桂成 Kaye Chon

田桂成，香港理工大学酒店及旅游业管理学院（SHTM）国际酒店管理专业的院长兼讲座教授以及郭氏基金会教授。

Prof. Kaye Chon is Dean and Chair Professor and Walter Kwok Foundation Professor in International Hospitality Management of the School of Hotel and Tourism Management at the Hong Kong Polytechnic University.

邱咏筠 Winnie Chiu

邱咏筠，太平绅士，拥有伦敦大学国王学院的商业管理学士学位，现任帝盛酒店集团总裁及执行董事、远东发展有限公司执行董事以及 Agora 酒店集团有限公司董事长。

Ms. Winnie Chiu, JP holds a BSc from King's College, University of London and currently is the President & Executive Director of Dorsett Hospitality International, Executive Director of Far East Consortium International Limited and the Chairman of AGORA Hospitality Group Co., Ltd .

何超琼 Pansy Ho

何超琼，信德集团有限公司集团行政主席兼总经理。

Ms. Pansy Ho is Group Executive Chairman and Managing Director of Shun Tak Holdings Limited.

吕耀东 Francis Lui Yiu Tung

吕耀东，嘉华集团副主席、香港上市公司嘉华国际集团有限公司执行董事和银河娱乐集团副主席。

Mr. Francis Lui Yiu Tung is Vice Chairman of K. Wah Group, Executive Director of Hong Kong-listed K. Wah International Holdings Limited, and Deputy Chairman of Hong Kong-listed Galaxy Entertainment Group (GEG).

亚洲是全球发展速度最快的旅游区（PATA，2019）。中国一直是亚洲地区经济增长的主要推动力，中国境内以及出入境旅游业都在以前所未有的规模增长。中国的影响力不仅仅体现在游客数量和旅游业的投资建设上，作为习近平主席"一带一路"倡议的一部分，中国正影响着丝绸之路经济带和21世纪海上丝绸之路沿线的国家。面对中国日益扩大的影响，如何投资与管理快速增长中的旅游业成为一项颇具挑战性的议题，需要及时了解中国国内外酒店业领导者所采取的战略。在这样快速增长的背景下，能引领新一轮浪潮的人势必被寄予更大的期望（Smith & Sigauw, 2011）。

本书起初是基于三位作者在培养和扩展中国酒店业领导力方面的共同兴趣而写的。这三位作者都在香港理工大学酒店及旅游业管理学院（SHTM）执教，他们的观点是在长年的酒店管理专业本科和研究生教学以及在酒店管理人员的培训中形成的。他们之前撰写过酒店业和旅游业方面的书籍，其中包括对行业领导者的采访，以期获得深入见解。笔者认为SHTM是本次调查的理想出发点。首先，本书涉及的研究经费是由该学院资助的。其次，该学院由院长田桂成教授领导，他率先提出了旅游和酒店业"亚洲浪潮"的概念和"亚洲范式"的概念（Chon 2014, 2018）。田院长作为本书的主要采访嘉宾和合作者之一，他的参与使酒店教育的观念更加得以深入，这是对领导力理念的探索，也是对新兴的亚洲领导力"最佳实践"的定义。

本书聚焦中国，旨在让读者从各位杰出人物的发言中探索领导理论和实践。

为了突出中国视角的核心地位，笔者用双语开展本书的写作。这一方面是受到笔者对中国学生双语教学经验的启发。通过15年前与浙江大学建立的合作关系，香港理工大学可以向学生授予酒店及旅游业管理理学硕士学位和酒店及旅游业管理博士学位（D.HTM），这些学生通常是经验丰富的行业高管。他们的平均从业经历长达9年，学习方式类似于高管教育。各学科教授均以中文授课，但书面材料是中英双语形式。多年来，这种高水平的酒店业研究生教育在中国各地形成了广泛的校友网络。一些校友为协助本书的完成接受了采访。这些部分建立在本书其中一位作者的论文的基础上，该论文提出了提高酒店业的专业水平的概念（Cheng and Wong, 2015）。

鉴于旅游业的快速增长，笔者证明了深入理解当前酒店业领导战略的必要性。如果要将这种势头持续下去，就必须了解现任领导者的相关见解。本书通过向读者展示对大中华区酒店和旅游业领导者所采用的创新方法的见解来阐明这些议题。

本书包括一系列对行业领导者的采访，这些采访都以双语方式呈现。本书的每一章都来自对行业领导者的采访录音整理。笔者、采访人采用了基于常见问题的半结构化采访方式，能够根据不同的环境和每个采访嘉宾的需求和偏好调整采访范围。访谈地点根据受访者偏好，选在不同的办公室，并以英文或中文进行。除一例通过电话会议进行的采访外，所有采访都是面对面进行的。受访者在各自的领域中都是高管（首席级别），通常是首席执行官、主席、创始人或副总裁。

由于个人领导力特征和企业因素之间有着紧密联系，笔者阐释了企业结构对行使领导力的影响。笔者还希望展现男女领导者的不同视角。九位采访嘉宾中包含四位女性和五位男性。这对于未来的企业领导者来说是一个重要的问题，因为目前酒店业大多数（70%）学生都是女性，所以了解她们面临的挑战和机遇至关重要。

作为一项科学研究，笔者首先试着浏览有关酒店业领导力的文献，之后从中国的酒店管理研究生群体中寻求关于领导力的见解，其中大多数人在管理酒店公司方面有着丰富的经验。为了进行试点研究，笔者在杭州和深圳进行了一系列专题小组访谈。这些访谈的报告已记录在学术文献中（Cheung, King and Wong, 2018）。作为刊登本项研究部分成果的杂志，笔者也将《旅游研究》杂志（JCTR）作为研究对象。JCTR 在 200 多家酒店和旅游学术期刊中独树一帜，其所有论文摘要均以中文和英文呈现。Cheung 等人的论文从中层管理者的视角分析了在中国最受尊敬的几位酒店高管，并确定了适应中国国情的领导力特质和特征。

依据对产业未来所投入时间和资源的不同，将受访者划分为不同的专题小组。这些高瞻远瞩的领导者对未来的看法尤其有趣，因为他们为了更好地领导酒店，越来越重视体验学习（Jian and Cheung, 2013）。之前的文献表明，他们所偏爱的管理活动将提供潜在有价值的见解（Waryszak and King, 2001）。由于香港理工大学酒店及旅游业管理学院内地校友队伍在不断壮大，而且越来越具有影响力，我们亦感到他们对领导力的看法可以对酒店管理教育的未来提出有价值的见解。

根据各专题小组的调查结果，笔者设置了以下问题作为主要调查主题，以求从受访者处获得最佳见解：

各位受访者是如何走上领导位置，并如何应对竞争的？

受访者认为新一代中国旅游业领导者将面临哪些挑战？

受访者所代表的酒店和旅游部门的领导特质是什么？

不同的公司类型会如何塑造领导力，特别是在国有企业、家族企业和跨国公司中？

受访者所在的公司如何顾及来自不同种族、文化和地域背景的客户和业务合作伙伴的偏好？

随着当前领导者阶层逐渐让位给新一代（千禧一代），培养接班人和世代变革方面是否存在挑战？

本书希望通过向读者提供受人尊重的高管关于个人和公司的经验之谈和深刻见解，激发行业从业者、学生和学者的兴趣。

金博蓝

2021 年 1 月

目录

Content

国有企业酒店的领导挑战

受访者：陈雪明先生
职　位：南京金陵酒店管理公司总裁
采访者：黄志恩博士

采访者：陈先生，能否谈一谈您进入酒店业的动机？

受访者：我的从业经历很有意思，我于1978年5月15日参加工作，最开始在上海的锦江饭店当西点师。那是家历史悠久的高档饭店，我在那儿工作了五年半后，进了中国最早的旅游专科学校——上海旅游高等专科学校学习。毕业后又回到锦江饭店做共青团委书记。之后，我获得了政府奖学金，赴德国留学两年，专攻酒店管理。1989年留学归来，我回到锦江饭店做市场营销工作，一步步从销售经理做到了CEO。我曾在上海锦江饭店、北京国际饭店、上海龙柏饭店、上海国际会议中心大酒店、上海光大会展中心等酒店担任副总经理、总经理和法人代表。此外，我还担任过两家房地产公司的董事。我于2011年3月正式加入南京金陵酒店管理公司，任总裁一职，目前在酒店业已工作近39年。

采访者：您是如何进入酒店业的？为什么要选择这个行业？

受访者：最开始是政府分配进酒店业的，我是在德国汉堡的四季酒店实习后，才下定决心成为职业酒店经理人。汉堡的四季酒店是全球最顶尖的酒店之一，可以说是欧洲最好的酒店。实习期间我深受触动，我觉得德国人可以管理好酒店，中国人为什么不可以。这个想法一直激励着我，我后来经营、管理过各类酒店，有大型的国际酒店、特色精品酒店、会议酒店、展览酒店、贵宾楼等。在具备了丰富的单体酒店经营管理经验后，我选择加入金陵酒店管理公司，开始做连锁酒店管理。

我最自豪的是在两个城市为两场国宴做总指挥。第一场是1999年江泽民总书记与财富 500 强企业代表在上海的国宴，第二场是 2014 年南京青奥会，习近平主席和李克强总理参加的国宴。这次国宴筹备过程艰苦，我压力很大，但是这个机会和经历非常难得。

采访者： 什么一直激励着您呢？

受访者： 是一种民族情怀在激励着我不断前进。20 世纪 80 年代初，中国酒店业还十分落后。我在德国学到了很多。在汉堡的四季酒店实习时我对两件事情记忆犹新。第一件事是四季酒店从不打折，因为他们坚信酒店的服务不打折扣，所以价格也不应打折。这意味着酒店价格取决于服务质量。另一件事是，某天有位客人没有预约就走到前台询问是否有空房，酒店实际上是有空房的，但经理告诉他已经订满了。我很惊讶，问经理为什么，经理没有直接回答我，而是反问道："你认识他吗？"我立刻明白了，这是全球顶尖的酒店，通过精准的市场定位明确了目标客户，不属于目标客户群体的，不接待也罢。我用这两套方法经营锦江龙柏饭店和锦江贵宾楼时都大获成功，经营得比外籍经理人还好。

我实习的另一家酒店是德国 Best Western 酒店。四季酒店有 145 间客房和 400 名员工，而这家酒店有 105 间客房，却只有 18 名员工，但仍然能提供优质的服务，这是将酒店的成本控制到了极致，说明员工数量并不是决定酒店经营成功与否的关键。我准备将这个策略用到金陵酒店管理公司近期准备打造的子品牌上。我一直想让国内酒店借鉴四季酒店和 Best Western 酒店的经营模式，以此推出我们自己的经营模式，锦江世纪城采用了四季酒店的模式，而金陵的子品牌将采用 Best Western 酒店的模式，我的梦想也算是实现了。国内酒店品牌在一线城市的表现可能不如国际品牌酒店，但在二三线城市的表现将实现超越。

采访者： 您能否总结一下酒店业领导力的主要特点？

受访者： 所谓领导力，就是让别人帮忙做你想做的事。我认为管理的最大成本是信任。酒店业客户关系管理的目标就是赢得信任，尤其是要赢得员工的信任，一旦获得他们的信任，你的领导或管理就将获得成功。这种信任不是靠职权获得的，而是靠"善"赢得的。酒店不是高科技行业，酒店工作更多的是处理好人际关系。一切酒店工作都绕不开处理关系，而良好的关系就是生产力。只有赢得员工的信任才能处理好各种关系。信任的背后包含各种要素，而成功领导的关键在于获得和维持团队成员的信任。

采访者：酒店业领导与其他行业的领导有什么不同？您是如何获得团队信任的？

受访者：酒店业和其他行业的不同之处在于，我们更加需要待人接物、处理关系的能力。我们要看人说话，根据情境灵活应对。酒店业实际上是让每个从业者都感到愉悦的行业，需要的是通才而不是专才。我有时候训斥下属，但他们也不会生气，因为他们知道这是出于"善意"。和我共事时间长了，他们知道我有三个原则：一是不给员工穿小鞋，二是不扣工资福利，三是有好的机会一定会想着员工。

采访者：作为酒店业的领导者，您是否面临过一些特别的挑战？

受访者：一是在这行要有待人接物的能力，能够处理好人际关系。二是除了专业知识外，还要认清酒店行业和企业的本质。虽然每个酒店都有共性，但也有各自的特性，所以要找到酒店的个性差异在哪儿，透过现象看本质。对这个企业认知的深度，决定了对这个企业的经营管理能否成功。

采访者：您 2011 年进入金陵酒店管理公司，在您看来，金陵与锦江在特性上有哪些差异？

受访者：改革开放至今，中国的酒店业发展迅速，新酒店纷纷成立，也有很多外资酒店进入中国市场，但总体而言，酒店管理公司却不太成功。不论是锦江还是金陵，它们其实都不算成功。究其原因是我们混淆了集团（group）和连锁（chain）的概念，没有透过现象来看本质。锦江属于集团，是以资本为纽带形成的大型酒店集团，也就是说这个企业的财务归在一个财务报表里面；而连锁是每个酒店有各自的报表，我们提供经营模式，只收管理费。我认为目前中国人还没理解这个区别。打个比方，单体酒店需要研究的是一杯水是倒六分还是七分好，而连锁酒店研究的是如何让连锁酒店的水符合统一标准。

"德鲁克三问"的第一问就是了解自己的企业，只有在深刻理解企业的个性和要求后才能走得更远。信任是最基本的，专业是基础，可以慢慢积累，此外，总经理还要会合理监督工作，很多总经理不会监督工作。管理其实就是下发任务单，任务单怎么发就反映出了领导力和管理能力。

至于用人，我的观点是韩信点兵，多多益善。没有刻意要哪种人，人才可遇不可求，一个只会打好牌的人，反而会束缚自己。不管手上的一套牌如何，你都可以打牌。每个人都有可塑性，重要的是用人所长、避人所短。能否取得成功要看领导是不是能够知人善用。当根据个人能力来分配工作时，我不认同赏罚分明，因为这样做的前提是定义工作完成的好与坏，这个界限很模糊，容易产生争议，导致谁重要、谁不重要的争论，使企业管理陷入混乱。

采访者：您最欣赏的酒店与旅游业领导者是谁？

受访者：我最欣赏侣海岩，他是警察出身，后被公安局派驻到酒店做副总，曾任北京昆仑饭店的总经理和中国旅游饭店协会会长，现已退休。他从外行一步步成为专家，是个奇才，也是个全才，写的小说还被拍成了电视剧。他身上最值得学习的地方是对酒店经营和人性管理的独到见解。他对下属的管理属于关爱型，严格又有情义，令我十分佩服。

采访者：您觉得国有企业与民营企业有何不同？

受访者：民营企业和国有企业的领导风格完全不一样。国有企业需要按照上级的规则来办事，不强求创新和效率，更不强求做事雷厉风行，最大的要求就是不犯错。哪怕十件事情有九件做对了，只要有一件出了错，都是不行的。因此，国有企业的领导需要具备按规矩办事的能力，国有企业是合规优先，而民营企业是效益、效率优先。金陵酒店管理公司虽然是市场化运营，但属于国有性质，所以我要做好协调工作，处理好效率和不出错之间的平衡。这是我面临的最大挑战。我要关注效益和效率，但在上报的环节中只要有一环卡住，就无法推行。每个人的出发点和考虑的角度都不同，想法很难统一，而且国有企业还要以国家政策为指导，而民营企业只要遵循相关法律和内部流程规范就行。

采访者：您是怎么带领团队引领市场的？

受访者：我认为只要在某一方面出类拔萃即可。以前金陵开了一个特许加盟模式运营的快捷连锁品牌"金一村"，整体市场形象混乱。考虑到公司经营能力有限，我就采取聚焦战略，使用单一品牌"金陵"，放弃特许加盟模式，采用单一经营模式"委托管理模式"，统一投资方针为"不投资而只做轻资产连锁管理"。此后，金陵的市场形象更加清晰，人们一想到金陵就知道是高端酒店，该市场定位目前受到了行业内的一致认可，成为本土连锁酒店争相效仿的典范。

采访者： 领导力如何传承给下一代？

受访者： 首先，作为领导要以身作则，处处展现出对这个行业的热爱，用自己对酒店业的热忱感染别人。其次，需要传递对酒店的认知、传递善。我每年都会在集团内做几次主题演讲，将自己对酒店的认知分享给下属，用善言善行影响别人。我们希望团队要亲善，这也是金陵所倡导的"金陵一家亲"原则。最后，领导者还要有启发他人处理问题的能力。专业知识是可以通过学习积累的，但领导力更多是修炼和感悟出来的，而不是在教室里学出来的。

采访者： 您如何形容金陵的企业文化？

受访者： 我们金陵酒店有自己特色的企业文化。我一直认为教育很重要，但是领导力不是通过演讲学出来的，不然，为什么接受同样的教育，同一个班就几个人出类拔萃呢？我们应该在课堂外多实践，所以我总是启发团队成员，启发比教育更重要。

采访者： 您认为酒店业的挑战是什么？

受访者： 我认为主要挑战就是文化冲突。比如，中国人比较含蓄，外国人是直线式思维，中国人讲究面子，外国人不讲究。因为这种文化上的冲突，我们一味地派人学习西方那套酒店管理是远远不够的。在和国际接轨的一线城市，聘请外籍管理人员或许还行得通，但到了二三线城市，基本上外籍管理人员全部撤了，酒店都在采用本土化战略，这就是因为有文化冲突。我一直提倡本土化，当地人管理当地市场是最好的。如果不具备文化理解的基础，是管不好跨区域酒店的。

采访者： 未来领导者的最大挑战是什么？

受访者： 领导者最大的挑战是需要具有非常强的融合能力。在连锁酒店做职业经理人，需要带领一个多元化的团队，大家背景各不相同，价值观也有差异，而领导者必须把他们团结在一起，让大家求大同、存小异。如果领导者没有这种融合能力，就需要对企业做出变革。融合是在不放弃个性前提下的兼容并包。

采访者： 您觉得领导的创新能力重要吗？

受访者： 我觉得对于领导而言，创新能力不是最重要的。一般企业分三类人：基层员工、专家和领导。所谓术业有专攻，创新更多是由专家负责。乔布斯也不是个创新者，他的成功之处在于他从 1000 个项目里选了 3 个项目，并且赢得了大家的认可，这不是他自己创新的。创新是专家的责任，领导更多的是进行上层管理，妥善地融合、管理团队。

采访者： 全球化给中国酒店业带来了什么挑战？

受访者： 中国的经济型酒店已经发展得较为成熟，但高端连锁酒店仍然是外资的天下，我们在这方面的认知还很落后，很少有人触及。中国最缺的是属于自己的轻资产高端奢华连锁酒店品牌，这对我们来说是巨大的挑战。职业经理人和资本拥有者站在不同的角度看待问题，职业经理人不是合适的投资人选，而资本拥有者更多考虑的是自有资产的增值能力，他们对连锁和集团的认知仍然停留在表面形式上，还未看透连锁的本质。

采访者： 性别问题、新生代员工、人口老龄化的问题对您的企业有影响吗？

受访者： 酒店行业是朝阳行业，只要有人的流动，酒店业就不会消亡。市场是根据供求关系调节的，虽然我们一直说酒店缺人，但是酒店依旧经营着，从业者薪酬不断提高，总能吸引到合适的人选，所以薪酬不用考虑。酒店业实际上是更适合女性的行业，投资可能更适合男性，但论经营管理和待人接物，女性会比男性更加细致到位。关于领导力的问题，总有人愿意做领导者。此外，我认为企业只有先让员工满意，才可能让顾客满意。

采访者： 国有企业的特点是什么？

受访者： 在国有企业里，领导力是弱化的，职务的高低决定了个人领导力。像我现在这样，职位够高时都不需要领导力，用行政能力就可以了。国企更多讲究的是规矩，在中国有个说法，枪打出头鸟，做事要低调，有魅力的、领导力很强的管理者在中国结果可能并不好。作为国有性质的企业，金陵面临的最大挑战是市场化和企业性质的协调。在我的工作中，有时既不能全讲合规，也不能全讲效率效益。例如，我们想成立下属公司，但是国家规定国有控股企业是无法成立四级公司的。如何协调呢？我把这个下属公司作为常规合作项目，签订合作协议，但实质上还是用公司运作的模式。这样虽然比较勉强，但是可以将事情做成。

采访者： 学习能力是不是也是构成领导力的重要因素？

受访者： 当然，学习是第一要务。领导者要紧密关注国际变化，要学习如何灵活应变，要看书、看文章了解变化的过程和原因，学习后还要进行深入思考。

跨界领导的秘诀

受访者： 金杜女士
职　位： 宛若故里创始人
采访者： 黄志恩博士

采访者： 您是如何从媒体转行酒店业的？

受访者： 我从本科到研究生都是新闻专业的，研究生时期就拿了新闻工作者优秀成果的最高荣誉奖韬奋新闻奖。还没毕业，我就被分到了南方日报集团，在那里工作了 15 年，是集团的重点培养对象。

第一点是兴趣。我转入酒店业是凭借个人兴趣。我认为发自内心热爱一件事是非常重要的，我知道自己就是喜欢酒店业，而喜欢一件事就会尽力把这件事做好。招聘时，我也只会招喜欢旅行、热爱交流的候选人，如果没有这种热忱，我是不会招进来的。

第二点是时机。当时我在报社工作了 15 年，职位已经很高了，我觉得我在传媒领域已经有足够的积累，触到了天花板，而且感觉媒体行业在走下坡路。

第三点是想要尝试新事物，业余时做点不一样的事，所以我和五个朋友在云南洱海边投资了一家民宿。从选址到签合同、装修、开张，项目进行得很顺利，入住率达 95%，人气很高。这个项目拿到了今年的中国最佳设计小而美酒店奖，这让我比赚到钱更开心。

民宿业为我进入酒店业提供了契机。我的主要目的并不是为了赚钱，"读万卷书，行万里路"一直是我没有改变过的人生信条。我认为教育能开拓人的大脑，旅行能开拓人的认知，所以我倾向于投资教育和旅行。后来，我发现当下的民宿业既没有一个领导型的品牌，也没有既定的规则，我就很好奇自己成功的民宿商业模式能否复制，便把民宿业确定为自己的早期创业方向。学习酒店业相关的理论也是一个动机。担任南都旅游事业部的总经理时我问黄老师我要不要去创业？黄老师建议我读个研究生。所以我为创业理念和模式做了一些准备：首先，我做了演示并获得了成功；其次，我在香港理工大学进修酒店管理课程，学习酒店业从业者的思维方式和相关理论；最后，我是一名经验丰富的记者，所以我的优势在于能够和行业专家接触，快速进入一个行业。我的朋友也建议我进入酒店和旅游行业，因为我的思维方式和一般人完全不一样，擅长解决问题。我给自己的民宿品牌提出了五个一的模式：一个故乡人，一群人的美宿，一次旅行，一个物产和一个故里社群，并获得了璎珞和铂涛的投资。

采访者： 酒店业和其他服务业领导者有什么特征？这些特征和其他行业的领导者有什么不同？

受访者： 本质差不多，都是如何激励员工和团队。但是不同行业的最佳实践也不同，比如以前在报社，大家都是高级知识分子，自我管理能力很强，于是企业管理就比较松散。但是酒店行业属于劳动密集型行业，员工平均受教育程度较低，这对我而言是个很大的挑战。因为我推崇员工自我管理，反对无效加班，希望大家高效工作、认真生活。我们做的是高体验型产品，只有认真体验生活，才能知道哪些点能打动客户。

其实我在创业的时候，人力资源上面临很大挑战，很难招到合适的人。许多人创业时都找自己的亲朋好友帮忙，但我在广州没有亲戚朋友，所以不得不寻找其他方法解决问题。我们公司每个人都很崇拜我，很认同企业文化。首先，我很有感染力，我招的员工要有很强的自我驱动力，要有很具体的梦想，比如想开个酒店或者想要到这里来向我学习。我希望宛若故里能变成一个平台，让大家分享财务资源、招聘方式和管理风格，帮助像我这样的人实现梦想。我的规则是客户体验永远放在第一位，我可以和员工分利润，但绝不能出现用户投诉。我们注重客户的感受，所以所有推荐的产品都有严格的审核。我招的都是价值观一致的人，我们对店长要求很高。另外，我的公司也注重创新。每年年初我会为员工制作一个今年的成长计划，比如员工如果希望薪资上浮，就需要多承担任务。我也允许员工在淡季休假，让他们通过旅行得到社交机会，增强应变能力。

采访者： 国有企业和私营企业的领导力特征差别大吗？个人因素和组织因素哪个对领导力的影响更大？

受访者： 我最早也是被主编的个人魅力吸引，进入南方报业集团的。他说，我们不是写文章，而是在改写社会进程。年轻人确实需要有梦想，没有梦想很难在工作中找到价值感，会觉得工作很枯燥无味。我认为梦想的力量是非常重要的，而且经历过痛苦和挑战，团队的凝聚力会更强。

后来因为组织规模扩大，管理流程越来越繁复，关键绩效指标考核更加频繁，我不是很喜欢。我希望我的公司里正式员工永远都不要超过 50 个人，我相信人少的公司也能创造高销售额，关键在于组织模式怎么创新。此外，我觉得业务和管理取得成功的关键是要对人性有深入的洞察。

采访者： 您最佩服的行业领军人物是谁？

受访者： 铂涛的创始人郑南雁。他从信息产业转到酒店业，和一群没有酒店业从业背景的人一起经营酒店。他提出企业永远处于微乱的状态是最健康的，这点我也非常赞同，因为微乱状态说明企业一直在创新。我很佩服他，因为我觉得真正的创业者很孤独，创始人和领导者既要克制自己，也要激励自己，这样的压力不是任何人都能承受的，所以我需要和其他创业者沟通交流。

我认为郑南雁能够透过现象看本质，迅速地捕捉他人的想法。他曾邀请我加入铂涛，我拒绝了，他就提出要投资我的公司，于是我问了他三个问题：

第一个问题是为什么要接受他的投资。他说："铂涛想持有更多股份，这是企业行为，但是从创始人的角度来说，我能够理解你的想法。为了打消你的顾虑，铂涛只占股 10%，我们不需要领导宛若故里，宛若故里也不用进入铂涛体系。"这番话打消了我的疑虑。

第二个问题，我问他："你投资我的公司对我有什么好处？"他说："当你顺利的时候对你没有任何的好处，但是你不顺利的时候铂涛可以帮你背书。"我觉得他说话非常坦诚中肯、一针见血。

第三个问题，我问他："对我有什么要求？"他说："没有什么要求，就是希望你每隔 2~3 个月和铂涛的高管互动一下。我们高管知道很多人的思维方式是不一样的，我之所以投资你，就是因为你的思维方式和我们不一样。也许有很多盲点我们看不到，但你能看到。"他做决策很迅速。

我是学者型创业者，这是我最大的优点，也是缺点。我做决策前总想征询他人意见、学习课程和（或）写商业计划书。郑南雁和我说，创业不是靠纸上写出来的，也不是靠商业计划书做出来的，我之所以这样是因为不敢创业，害怕失败。创业是无数次失败积累出来的，不是从纸上推演出来的。

有位天使投资人说我最大的优点是能在短时间内掌握某个行业的整体现状，但这可能导致我思虑过多，欠缺行动力。

自我认知对实现高效领导来说非常关键。我们要了解自己的长处和短板。我们公司招聘时用的是贝尔宾团队角色表。我们认为不可能有完美的人，但是可以有完美的团队。一个团队需要有各种成员：办事谨慎的、创意无限的等。我们试图发现别人的优点和不足，然后决定适合的岗位。比如有人很爱找出问题，可以安排其去做流程监控；有人想法多，就可以去做营销，绝不能去做财务。为了减轻团队成员的压力，我给他们安排的 70% 的任务是他们擅长的事情，另外 30% 的任务是他们所不熟悉的。

采访者： 您成功的秘诀之一就是发挥他们的优势，不要施加过多压力吗？

受访者： 如果任务的难度过大，团队成员很容易陷入自我否定。年轻人在工作中最想获得的是成就感，这比钱更重要。如果直接告诉他们该怎么做，他们可能不开心，他们更乐于自己去尝试，如果通过自己的努力获得成功，他们就会很开心。团队的吸引力与钱和老板的魅力无关，最重要的是让员工通过工作变得越来越自信。

采访者： 您是怎么看待关系的？

受访者： 现在的商业环境和以前不同，我们公司完全不靠关系，只要我站到台上说出我的理念，大家就乐于与我合作。我需要发挥自己的感染力。在和碧桂园的高管团队分享我的创业经历时，我讲了自己经历的坎坷和挑战以及我的价值观和理念。他们觉得我的想法和传统酒店的理念完全不一样。邀请我去做分享的是我的同学冀宏军，他认为我有值得和高管团队分享的想法，而我也从他们务实的做事风格和企业文化中受益，所以这次分享是双向的。他们企业很高效，执行能力强。

采访者： 宛若故里的企业文化是怎样的？

受访者： 宛若故里有自己的企业价值观。第一是用户体验至上，需要通过研究了解问题本质。第二是关注小事，毕竟大事也是由成百上千件小事构成的。第三是懂得与人分享，我从来不怕有人过来和我谈工资待遇。比如之前在南方报业，我带领几百人的销售团队，每年年初都会有销售人员来我办公室谈期望薪资。我会从资料库里找到 20 家没有开发过的客户，让他们研究一个月，明确哪些是潜在客户，再帮他们分析如何拿下这些客户，这就是实现了双方的共赢。我觉得同理心特别重要，要从员工的角度思考问题，也要从企业的角度思考问题。和消费者沟通要站在消费者的角度，我觉得只考虑股东权益的企业是走不远的。

采访者： 怎样让下一代领导者传承良好的领导力？

受访者： 我们还没有遇到这个问题。南方报业这样的国有企业有这个问题，最开始几任领导都是通过传承企业价值观实现成功的，但是现任领导并不认同以前的价值观，团队成员也很疑惑。国有企业最大的问题就是，接班人不是领导自己选择的，而是组织安排的，可能只待 3~5 年就走了，不会考虑企业价值观和百年传承的问题。企业文化通常能反映出领导者的个人风格，内敛型的领导者会着重高效执行，创新型领导者就会鼓励创新和冒险。在内地的国有企业里，领导者差异很大，这是一种领导者文化，而像碧桂园这样的民营企业，就更偏向家族文化。

采访者： 你们公司有继承计划吗？

受访者： 有的，我们公司员工不多，这个问题很好解决。我们都在一起工作，最重要的是道德品质。我们的文化很简单，不要挑拨是非。我认为自己是个很有原则的人，接受了我安排的任务，就要负责，如果答应了却没完成就会被惩罚。我认为一诺千金是很重要的，只有信守承诺，才能不影响别人。

采访者： 中国酒店目前主要面临什么挑战？

受访者： 我们公司有几个年轻人在传统酒店工作过，他们都没在五星级酒店工作过，因为在那里学不到东西。"90 后"的观念和老一辈不一样，他们不喜欢枯燥的工作，所以接下来酒店行业遇到的最大的挑战是让他们保持激情并获得成就感。"60 后""70 后"有强烈的责任感，但是"90 后"不一样，大多数人不想买房，想环游世界。他们注重和客户交流，喜欢做民宿是因为觉得更能当家做主。我们的店长都是 20 多岁的年轻人，我们这次策划了一个闺蜜私奔记，获得了环球女性创新奖。

采访者： 您是怎么想到做"闺蜜私奔记"的？

受访者：我们做事始终从用户角度出发。中国女性越来越注重个人成长和发展。我和朋友每年都要旅行，边旅行边交流经验。我觉得旅行体验是一个复合体验，我们可以边学边玩。所以我们提出这个概念，开放用户报名。在这次活动中，我们的店长表现都很突出，客人甚至都想留下来当店长了！

70%的日常消费品都是为吸引女性设计的，因为女性是关键决策者和购买行为的主体。我也是女性消费者，所以我很了解这个群体。虽然宛若故里的销售额并不高，但是它在这个行业里具有很高的知名度。对我而言，酒店业只是个平台，让我认识很多有趣的人。另外，我是一个资源的整合者，擅长整合各种各样的资源，尤其是在媒体行业。

我与年轻人相处融洽的原因是我给他们比较大的自主权。举例而言，我让他们完全负责设计行程，自己只是提意见。我允许他们犯小错误，大错误不行，而且犯错后要自己想方法弥补，不能重复犯错。如果不允许别人犯错，企业怎么能进步呢？年轻人有表现的欲望，喜欢享受成就感。在我的公司，他们有很多机会，只需要遵守60%~70%的标准操作程序，其他的都可以自行决定。如果希望加薪，可以来说服我，如果说服不了，就给其十天时间尝试一下。我觉得理解他们的需求、让他们追寻梦想十分重要，和卖产品一样重要。

采访者：您如何处理家庭关系，平衡家庭和工作之间的关系？

受访者：我和老公合理分工，他管家庭和孩子。但是有时他也会抱怨，觉得我的工作强度还是超过了他的想象。

我有自己的观点：用管理公司的方法管理一个家。我家人的执行力很强，他们负责执行，我只需要帮助他们设定目标，告诉他们怎么做。我给孩子做一个表格，安排他需要做的事情。他现在6岁，喜欢吃比萨。为了督促他达到目标，我和他约定只要他能达到我的要求，每周就请他吃一次比萨。比如一天要做7件事情，一周要做49件事，如果全部完成就能得到49分，如果有一件事没有完成，就要扣2分。如果一周得分达到或超过20分，他就可以吃比萨。每天要完成的7件事中，有5件是他擅长的，2件是不擅长的。现在他比我还自律。有时候我出差也会带上家人，我就觉得教育也是言传身教，看到妈妈很努力地工作，孩子也会努力学习，他的自我管理能力很强。

采访者：政府政策是如何影响你的领导方式的？

受访者： 我相信政府政策能影响领导方式和企业的最终收益。政策变化也会影响到企业领导。

采访者： 您认为成功的领导者需要具备什么重要特质？

受访者： 要开明大度。领导是否受欢迎取决于他们的胸怀和包容度。我们每个人的个性都不同，只用一种方法没法管理所有人。每个人都有长处和短处，如果领导有足够的胸怀，就能知人善用。仅凭智慧，没有胸怀是做不了好领导的。我之前即使冒犯了郑南雁，他也没有生气，这就是他的胸怀。

采访者： 未来的领导者需要有跨界能力吗？

受访者： 未必。领导者最重要的是透过现象看本质的能力，是洞察人性的能力。获得跨界能力主要是积累知识，但是知识和技能的壁垒相对较低，许多行业专家也都具备。洞察的能力很重要，有些人虽然有行业知识，但是不能跨界，就是因为他们没法发现问题的本质。比如我常常问员工，碧桂园为什么要和宛若故里合作？我们的竞争力不在于我们成本低，而在于我们的产品实现了差异化，这是个判断依据。采购人员优先考虑的是成本，我知道这点，所以会让他们思考“为什么碧桂园想和我们合作”。无非是因为我们的产品理念、概念和包装有很大的附加值，既然这样为什么还要削减成本、削弱我们的核心竞争力？看清这点就是在透过现象看本质。

弘扬中华传统文化　打造高档度假村品牌

受访者： 魏黎先生
职　位： WEI 品牌创始人
采访者： 黄志恩博士

采访者： 您为什么选择酒店行业？

受访者： 我找第一份工作的那个年代，酒店业也刚刚起步。我家在乌鲁木齐，我找工作时，乌鲁木齐唯一的国际企业——假日酒店（Holiday Inn）正好在招聘，当时这家酒店位于市里最高档的楼里，这楼的业主是旅游局。我觉得这是乌鲁木齐唯一一家国际酒店企业，就去应聘了。在接下来的 12 年里，我在洲际酒店工作，从最基层的服务员做起，慢慢在酒店业成长起来了。

采访者： 是什么一直激励着您从事酒店业？又是什么促使您从打工转向创业？

受访者： 我这个人一直很有上进心，做事持之以恒。我也始终追寻心之所向。发展到现在这个阶段，我想超越自己、挑战自己，而且从事服务行业让我不断成长，所以我一直想在这个行业做出贡献，帮助中国酒店品牌更加国际化。

采访者： 酒店领导者需要有什么特征？这些特征是否有别于其他行业？

受访者： 我举例说明一下，高科技行业需要年轻人，需要具有前瞻性思维的领导，而酒店行业需要不同的领导者，酒店业的模式更像是一个家庭，需要代代传承，即使是世界五百强的酒店也不例外。例如，同是世界五百强企业，万豪酒店集团是企业家族化管理模式，已经传承了三代，而中国的美的空调是职业经理人在打理，两者都是全球知名企业，为什么会采用不同的管理经营模式？我认为还是因为行业不同。美的空调要做产品，需要对理念和流水线系统进行不断快速创新，每个阶段的任务都不同，而酒店服务行业更像是个大家庭，所以两者的领导力形式不同。

采访者：您的领导风格是什么？

受访者：我特别注重细节，思维缜密，坚强有毅力，而且追求卓越。我自己是从基层起家的，所以我会特别关注细节、逻辑思维和系统思维。早在20年前，我在做管事部经理的时候，就会仔细盘点整个库房、餐具用具，统计每年的预算、储藏室和购买期。我的逻辑思维很强，会把控细节，这就是我平时的行事和思考方式。

采访者：您是如何让企业在奢侈酒店品牌市场中脱颖而出的？

受访者：首先，我很熟悉中国市场，有着20多年的从业经验，先后任职于洲际酒店集团、香格里拉、雅高集团、悦榕庄和华侨城集团，所以非常了解国际品牌和国内市场状况。其次，通过过去30年中国经济及酒店业的不断发展我觉得现在是合适的时间来创立中国人自己的国际酒店品牌。我是酒店人，我用自己的姓氏创立品牌，我想帮助更多业主并得到大家对行业的信任。

采访者：能介绍一下WEI这个品牌吗？您在创立这个品牌时，产品营销和管理模式都加入了很多中国元素。您为什么会有这样的产品构想？

受访者：我读了很多关于万豪、希尔顿、凯宾斯基酒店的书，这些酒店名用的都是创始人的姓氏。读完后，我发现全球酒店业近百年的游戏规则都是由外国的八家老牌酒店制定的，五个美国的（万豪、希尔顿、喜达屋、凯悦和温德姆），一个法国的（雅高），一个英国的（洲际），还有一个德国的（凯宾斯基），它们制定的规则和标准基于西方文化。我从古代和现代的中国文化史了解到，中国在3000年前就引领世界超过500多年，唐宋时期的古人就已经开始注重奢华、艺术、设计、文化、美食、享受，清朝宫廷有满汉全席。所以我认为，中国对文化和奢华服务的注重由来已久，我们应重塑中国古老的服务和文化，针对现代快速发展的社会需求做出调整。中国有五千年的历史，可以算是一位"长者"，而西方相对而言是"快速成长的年轻人"，"长者"的生活阅历、文化底蕴显然更为深厚。然而，现在在我们需要把古老的文化以更具活力、更加现代的方式展现出来，让全球的客人体验和感受。总之，我觉得中国的服务业将走向世界，于下一个世纪在全球行业范围内发挥重要引领作用。

因此，我也用了自己姓氏的拼音WEI作为品牌名，还把WEI设计成了《周易》中的卦作为品牌标志：W成了三竖，代表着众生，E成了三横，代表着天、地、人，I 成了一竖，代表着家庭和孝顺。从玄学来看，三三得九，九九归一，一生二，二生三，三生万物，卦相包含无数含义。《周易》中载录了六十四卦，分别属金、木、水、火、土五行，每卦对应的位置不同，天地人也会有不同的运势。中华文化有几千年的历史、博大精深，我认为我们需要融入这些文化元素，所以我选择以这种方式，将我的姓氏作为酒店名，给予对服务的承诺，同时传递不一样的东方优雅。

此外，品牌还融合了中国传统禅、茶和医的元素。禅、茶、医贯穿中国千年历史，带来高级的奢华阅历，医代表着中医的养生之道。我的产品追求的不是资本注入，而是精神层面的升华。百善孝为先，我们倡导的是孝顺的传统，是尊老爱幼的中华品德，用"孝"字告诉中国年青一代如何善待、服务他人。每当我们的酒店分店开业时，我们只会邀请员工的父母参加开业仪式，我们要踏踏实实地用心服务我们的尊贵客人。未来中国将成为最大的旅游输出国，应有行业领军人才加入这个精英队伍，参与推动全球酒店业的变革。

采访者： 在打造品牌时融入了传统中国文化和元素，您认为主要挑战是什么？

受访者： 第一个挑战就是信任。近 200 年来，中国发生了太多变化，尤其是这 100 年，中国没有自己的奢华酒店品牌，所以没有自信、没有对创造力的积极认可。大家都想着怎么生存、怎么快速赚钱。当我在外宣传自己的品牌时，人们都不相信我，这确实也不意外。所以我觉得信任和信赖是最大的挑战。第二个挑战是当代年轻人的个性。在现有教育体系下，培养服务业人才很难，未来中国服务业从业人员规模将会扩大，但我们却没有完善的教育和培训体系来迎接快速发展的时代。总结一下，第一个挑战是获得业主和投资商的信任，第二个是重新设计适合中国及国际市场的服务体系。

采访者： 您的行业楷模是谁？

受访者： 我佩服万豪酒店的 J.W. Marriott, Jr。他的书我都读过，我觉得他真的是很努力地在与时俱进。我觉得他最打动我的是他坚守本心、工作努力，有企业家精神。他坚持扩大业务规模，把万豪酒店打造成全球最大的酒店之一。

采访者： 您眼中的中国酒店业是什么样？

受访者： 酒店管理行业和每个国家的管理制度有相同之处，也有独特之处。我觉得酒店业更像是一个小的"联合国"。每个国家的文化特点不同，且对于高、中、低档酒店服务的需求也不同。所以我认为，酒店业领导力是个全球通用的概念，酒店是一种文化和传承。

采访者： 对于酒店业而言，关系有多重要？

受访者： 我觉得关系是个积极的概念。全球各地的酒店人就像一家人一样，大家一同努力，变得更强大。有了网络，我们可以联系世界上任何角落的酒店人并建立关系，这样的关系是非常积极的。

采访者： 全球化对酒店人有什么影响？

受访者： 全球化给酒店与旅游业带来了特别的挑战。理想状况下，全球化应该会推动我们发展，但是全球发展实在太快了。我们的前辈知道我们是如何代代传承的，我们也希望能够平稳、顺利地传给下一代。然而，年青一代认为我们的想法过时了，所以我们需要考虑如何顺利、平稳地传承企业。

采访者： 您的企业全球扩张时，文化因素是否产生了一些影响？尤其是"一带一路"战略，是否带来了什么挑战？

受访者： 我在格鲁吉亚开了两家酒店，还有一家酒店在筹备开张阶段，在日本北海道已经开业一家酒店，接下来还会有四家开业，在迪拜准备开一家酒店，我们计划明年在欧洲开 4~5 家酒店。实话说，我没觉得是特别大的挑战。我在外企待了 20 多年，我待过的企业都有百年历史，沿用欧洲那套标准体系和多年积累的方法。这 20 多年来，中国在快速发展的阶段使用到最好的硬件、软件、食品、设计等，能提供最好的工艺，是应该向世界分享我们学习到的经验了。中国现在成了最大的旅游输出国，国力日渐强大。所以当我跨出国门、拓展海外业务时，我觉得要给行业分享我们的经验。我们需要创新，需要引领潮流，而不是执着于保守的价值观和看法。

采访者： 您对香港和澳门的酒店有何看法？

受访者： 在中国内地，由于城市规模大，所以对酒店的需求属于刚需。虽然需求大，但是酒店业仍需要提高服务质量和从业人员素质。中国香港是国际化大都市，人员素质高，我认为我国香港酒店业的挑战是及时根据市场变化，调整市场策略，否则酒店收益将会受影响。我很看好澳门的酒店业，那里的产品符合中国现阶段的需求。除赌场外，澳门还有很多适合家庭入住的酒店，附近有很多可供家庭游玩的景点，因此我认为澳门酒店业未来的发展前景很好。

采访者： 您是怎么看待酒店与旅游业的领导力传承的？

受访者： 我们倾向认为"60后"和"70后"是领导的主力军。这些人都是外企或国有企业培养出来的，经验丰富，不过很快会退休。实际上，"80后"和"90后"在不久的将来将成为酒店业的主力军。"80后"生活条件相对比较好，年龄上适合当酒店的骨干。20世纪80年代末和90年代初的这一代人可能要从我们手中接过交接棒，把酒店业推向新高度。

采访者： 您认为新一代的酒店领导者会面临哪些挑战？

受访者： 新一代领导者的挑战来源于不断变化的客户群体。现在主要客户都是"90后"，企业需要根据他们的特性，调整产品服务和营销策略。然而，酒店行业中一些传统的元素还是不会改变，比如后台和运营。因此，我认为领导者的挑战是踏实地学习和提升自己。

采访者： 您如何看待员工的满意度？

受访者： 我认为员工的满意度很重要。在不同的城市、不同的时代，满意度也不一样。从我个人经历来看，员工餐、奖金、假期和礼品到位，老员工基本上就满意了，但是现在的年轻人不在乎这些，他们需要目标，需要一段时间来实现这个目标。这些年轻人家里的经济条件都不错，所以不太看重金钱，追求的是成就感和头衔。这和以前完全不同，所以我们也应制定新的标准。

采访者： 学习在您的职业发展中起到了什么作用？

受访者： 我喜欢做事持之以恒，乐于学习新知识，我认为学习至关重要。我喜欢挑战，做别人不敢做的事。我认为学习帮我梳理自己的思维，明确多年来我做了什么以及未来要做什么。我在香港理工大学进修后，分析思维和解决问题的方式都不一样了，能比以前更理性、客观地考虑问题。

采访者： 奢华酒店未来会怎么发展？

受访者： 高端市场是一定存在的，未来二三十年，中国的高端市场将会不断发展，尤其是在旅游住宿业。我认为，主题文化精品酒店将是接下来的发展机遇所在。

带领香港顶级酒店品牌　缔造全球骄人业绩

受访者： 郭敬文先生
职　位： 香港上海大酒店有限公司董事总经理及行政总裁
采访者： 金博蓝教授

采访者： 您的专业是财务会计，请问是什么促使您投身酒店行业呢？

受访者： 我觉得对所有管理人员来说，拥有足够的经验去应对不同情况并想办法解决难题最为关键，以往接受的会计、财务、法律或咨询顾问反而是次要的，不过，这些专业知识也会潜移默化地被用到。投身商界之初，我已觉得会计是较着重"回顾"的专业，主要是检核别人的工作记录，当时就想向比较讲求"即时性"的行业发展，也正是这种渴望推动了我加入银行界。在银行界工作，你可以即时与人交易，过程中涉及谈判，我认为这很有启发性，也是很宝贵的学习机会。

从事会计工作，做好文件记录是基本工作。在银行工作时，我认识到做生意其实无正式规则可言，你必须按既定目标并且公正合理地谈判，这是极好的训练。从长期的银行工作经验所得，我认为自己担当中间人角色，代表其他委托人进行交易，并要承担一些风险。无论做承销、就某件事表明立场或发布公开文件，要承担所有涉及的责任，就算事事谨慎尽责，也始终与经营自己的公司不同，管理自己的公司要承担全部责任。我觉得自己较适合管理企业，因为我较着眼宏观及长远的思考，性格又较保守，继续从事银行工作未必是长远之计，所以要找更好的事业发展机会。

港铁（香港铁路有限公司，MTR）是一个绝佳的机会，因为当时港铁在国际资本市场很活跃，在港铁做企业管理是我非常宝贵的经验。我也乐于接受挑战，因为可以在不同国际资本市场发行和谈判中丰富自己的经验。更重要的是，港铁的卓越管理制度令我获益良多。港铁管理流程顺畅高效，架构组织完善，一直严守最高的企业管理标准。当时港铁是重要的发行人，由香港特区政府全权拥有，我加入港铁积累企业管理经验也顺理成章。当了财务总监（CFO）一段日子，可以预期再进一步就是行政总裁（CEO）。以音乐作比喻，与其演奏乐器，不如去指挥管弦乐团。因为我认识嘉道理家族，大家相处融洽，所以有了出任 CEO 的机会。我当时并非视之为首选行业，而是觉得酒店业很有吸引力（至今观感依然），我考虑的是如何将财务及企业管理经验运用在其中。

说回管弦乐团的比喻，指挥要使每段乐章协调，就要让乐师发挥最好水准，要了解并利用他们的优点，建立良好关系，令其发挥得更好并明白如何精益求精。这个比喻说明一个好指挥必备的条件，虽然乐团最重要的始终是全体合作无间。虽然我从没在管弦乐团演奏过，但我认为一个差的指挥无法协调好乐师，乐师自然不满自己的演奏，也就无法奏出悦耳的旋律。

这指挥的比喻亦适用于酒店业：我自己不会拉小提琴或演奏其他乐器，不会烹煮美食，不会按年份挑选葡萄酒佳酿，也不懂客房室内装潢，所以要信赖专家的建议。酒店业这门生意，人际关系至关重要，而情感因素往往是与客人交流的重点。如果你跟自己人都无法好好沟通交流，那么与客人的互动想必多半徒劳无功。酒店业极依赖人与人的接触，我非常明白业务成败得失，并非因为我在办公室说了什么、做了什么，而是取决于员工日常互动以及跟客人的接触。由于酒店中每位员工都有自己的特殊才能，所以用乐团指挥比喻就很合适。在以人为本的企业里，领袖和管理人员必须协调运用这些不同技能。我们在对酒店的一流服务感到自豪的同时，也要透彻了解如何满足顾客对服务的期望。在西方国家最高级的酒店里，豪华客房的房价可能超过每晚 1000 美元（套房房价更是高得多）。有些顾客要求很高，你不仅要满足他们所有要求，更要预见他们需要什么，为他们创设独特、难忘的体验。客人买的是体验而非一个房间，酒店要花尽心思结合不同部门的努力，才能符合客人的期望。

采访者：哪些领袖特质在酒店业中特别重要？

受访者：不同行业人才的基本特质大同小异，说到底，各行业都追求业务表现及高效率管理。酒店业不同之处或在于能够较易吸引到有艺术气质或较感性的人才，而且这有正面作用，因为在酒店大堂或一个活动中，理应有让客人感到宾至如归的气氛。要做到这一点，需要勇气和跳出框框的思维。加入半岛酒店前，我在港铁与许多工程和建筑系毕业生共事。在香港上海大酒店，员工较讲求个性及自由发挥，专业会计师反而较少。我为集团带来了流程管理、架构制度及管理透明度，令同事有指引可循，并有机会透彻了解自己的角色和职能，进而将较艺术性及感性的处事方式融入有例可循的管理架构中。

采访者： 据观察，追求短期财务业绩是大型酒店集团的动力。您怎样兼顾协调公司的长期及短期目标？

受访者： 我认为无须对业绩期望及业务策略规定得太死，这样也可以避免业务过度增长，因为扩张到超过某个点，就需要引入新的合规和监管程序调整管理流程。虽然未必所有情况都完全兼顾"因时制宜"和"标准化"两种方针，但我会提倡同事要有正确的思维和心态。同事了解客人欢迎的产品和体验，结果就会在财务业绩中得到反映。我与集团的各位总经理会定期检讨业绩并商讨下一步工作计划，但亦会给他们相当大的自主权。我会视酒店总经理为凭实力做出成绩的生意人。

我非常重视企业的集体决策过程。我与集团管理理事会通力合作，委员会有9位成员，包括执行董事、集团人力资源、资讯科技等重要职能部门主管。我会这样概述自己的管理风格：我们做决策或寻求项目批核时，负责的部门（同事）会提交详尽文件说明所有重点，要关注的可能是财务、法律、技术、人力资源或企业社会责任的事项。负责的部门会参与其中，牵涉的部门包括非集团管理理事会成员会参与讨论，大家都明白讨论过程中应提出意见或问题。我未必会同意所有观点，如有异议会尽量解释理由，不过最终是由我做决定，但必须经刚才提及的全体参与和讨论后才做出，要经大家共同决策。如果出了什么问题，不会有人在半年过后回头说："其实我没有同意过，只不过我没说出来。"原则就是大家一起商议，这是我的决策风格。

而且我不擅长保守秘密，我会令同事了解公司的情况。我每个月都会同集团所有总经理开电话会议，各运营与职能部门的总经理都会参与电话会议，我会简报最新进展，避免事情不清不楚。有多达40人参加电话会议，分享最新发展动态，这就是我管理公司的重要原则。

采访者： 哪些领导或创新措施让你觉得特别为之自豪？

受访者： 从根本谈起，我对酒店的服务质量和优越位置最自豪，尤其是近年来的新酒店项目都能惠及当地社区。我对公司的社会责任、客房科技以及数码技术转型亦很满意。集团有自己的研发部门，负责研发我们专用的客房科技和电子设备。

采访者： 能否请您谈一谈香港业务的领导与运作？

受访者： 我在中国香港长大，在英国读的中学和大学。我的孩子在美国读的中学和大学。中国香港会聚世界各地来客，这种国际化文化环境令来港工作的外地人很容易适应。香港人长期接触外国人，与不同国家及文化背景的人士打交道都很有经验，而且经常出门，见多识广。香港人的教育背景也各不相同，大多接受过西方教育，不少香港人到英美读书，近年来也有不少人到内地和其他地方接受教育。香港得益于多元化的优势，你可以很有信心地在香港总部管理不同地区的业务，而且可以信赖团队的经验。如果你的团队和我的相似，总部同样在香港，那你不会担心某位同事是否有能力去法国或其他地方开会，因为你很清楚同事都成熟且世故，经验丰富。中国香港一直是会聚国际人才之地。

采访者： 香港商界是维护普世专业精神的中流砥柱吗？

受访者： 对。香港有很多受专业训练及良好教育的人才，这是香港的优势，而且香港有很完善的法律、会计和银行制度，我衷心希望这种优势能够保持下去。

我觉得我们有时会忘记香港的优势——香港人效率高、工作勤奋、技能多样、执行力强，实在不应妄自菲薄，我接受采访时经常鼓励大家要善用自己的优势。

采访者： 您初入职场是什么样的？

受访者： 我敬仰的人未必是乔布斯那种很有启发性的人物，相反，我最难忘的是职业生涯之初对我影响甚深的人。当初我在罗兵咸会计师事务所工作，还没拿到专业核数师资格。我工作才六个月就被派去核数，并被告知会有位高级经理来审查旧文件和已完成的工作。我那时毕业没多久，以为高级经理是个大人物，我要立正尊称他一句先生。我以为会见识到高层人士派头，类似国家总统那种。事实上他人很好，友善又有风度，但最重要的是他深入复核工作的细节。我以为高级经理层次很高，只会做全局考虑，这令我惊讶又钦佩。当时我很年轻，又初入职场，对一切了解不深，也没有真正考虑过自己的期望。而那位高级经理极重视细节，深入研究并能找出问题所在，对此我深受触动，可谓获益良多。

采访者： 全球化和中国的崛起如何影响酒店业领导？

受访者： 我会从广义层面回答这个问题。人向来都喜欢美好的事物，见到华丽的酒店套房和水疗中心就会想去享受，这几乎与人的出身背景无关。随着我们在世界各地拓展业务，接待越来越多不同背景的顾客，这实在不足为奇，亦很乐见，但要学习处理不同文化国籍人士的要求和想法。这涉及接触不同组群并向之宣传推广，妥善处理他们的要求，缔造美好的体验，这一点也不复杂。值得注意的是，"全球化"一词的使用已太普遍，但全球化也带来了安全、种族冲突和外交层面等问题，这会影响我们的管理方式，情况难免会变得更为复杂，但我们无法控制及左右这些问题的出现。

目前，集团部分业务受到政治与贸易问题的影响。我们做出投资决策后，就要长期坚持直至圆满成功。我们希望选择最合适的地点去发展，一旦落实就坚持下去，尽力处理好遇到的问题。幸好，我们公司的目光非常长远，且具备充足资源及正确心态处理这种不确定的情况，而我亦要根据全局和长远目标，规划发展蓝图。

采访者： 世代交替与技术变革的影响是什么？

受访者： 大家觉得年轻人和老年人全然不同。我之前提到，人天生渴望享受奢华，我觉得就算年岁渐长，这心态亦不会改变。我们都希望前途光明、前程似锦、事事顺利、自由满足。然而情况不断变化，现在的选择比从前多，有些事物以前很有吸引力，现在却已褪色不少。就业市场，特别是大家向往及接受的工种变化很大，新工种带来了新的工作形式。好像我儿子工作的地方，员工可以穿便装上班，他们努力工作，效率很高。我儿子很聪明、受过良好教育，喜欢可以穿便服的工作环境，而不是要求穿笔挺西装的酒店业。大家对于理想工作环境的选择已经改变，所以大家要适应可以提高生活质量的新事物，但不能放弃基本的服务原则，亦不能大幅度更改利润最高的产品。

某些行业会较容易适应。服务行业讲求纪律及特定的做事方法，我们对此进行了深入研究，我特别留意科技在加强通信从而改善生活质量的角色。同样，随着科技发展，许多工种已被淘汰，未来人可以做什么还是未知之数。以前，有人可以开一辈子的火车。我们注意到了这些变化。但正如之前提到，基本原则仍然不变，包括培养人才、技能，给他们有趣的挑战及事业发展机会，当然还有经济回报，令他们可以过像样的生活。尽管这些没有改变，但环境和方法手段已不尽相同。

采访者：科技这一点听起来很有趣，您可以详细讲解您的策略吗？我曾陪同一批酒店融资和专业技术人士参观香港半岛酒店，体会到酒店在利用新科技提升服务方面的努力。

受访者：我们采用演进而非革命性的方法，我们尊重传统，因传统是我们的优势之本，在了解及珍视往昔成就、传承集团价值观之余，还要了解世界如何改变。

采访者：贵公司总部摆放着各式徽章，是否代表要彰显集团丰富的传统？

受访者：你看看我的名片，会发现我们沿用原来的徽章标志，因为它代表集团的历史和传承，但用上新设计和配色，可塑造更有时代感的形象。虽然名片设计很传统，但希望你不会有半岛是家守旧的企业、不会与时俱进的印象。

采访者：您如何看待中国酒店业领导的"关系"观？

受访者：我认为领袖的风格与种族特性无关。我工作生涯中见过不同风格的领袖，这取决于公司背景和文化。众所周知，中国香港有许多家族企业靠自己的努力逐步建立起来，这是一种事必躬亲、亲力亲为的家族管理方式。相反，西方企业有独立董事局，股东与管理层分得很清楚。这些背景决定了不同的领导风格。我提过，有些中国公司是从大型国有企业转型而来，当中又有特定的价值观及共识。所以我觉得不同组织架构会孕育不同的领导方式，但个人领导风格始终由个人所定，特定的组织架构会有自己的领导方式和管理方式。

采访者：政府在香港经营企业中扮演的角色是什么？

受访者：我在银行工作时参观过许多中国内地企业，每当我请他们介绍一下公司的业务及前景时，对方都会回应类似的话："待我介绍你认识这位政府官员，你就会明白。"当时中国政府的政策和监管，很大程度上影响了企业的决策。很明显，香港的酒店业未受监管。我在港铁工作时，非常关心政府的交通运输和房屋政策。虽然香港酒店业不受监管，我们在海外经营业务多数要先得到规划批核，但多与批核程序有关而非政府政策。私人企业如有意收购一块地皮就会去谈判，这是商业运作的基本原则，政府政策对其的影响不大。如果政府推出有利经济及旅游业发展的政策，业界当然欢迎。

在关系型酒店环境中发挥领导力

受访者： 郑志雯女士
职　位： 瑰丽酒店集团首席执行官
采访者： 张玉艳博士

采访者： 您的集团组织内的有效领导有哪些特点？

受访者： 在酒店业，领导者必须关注"人"。服务业本质是以人为本的日常业务。酒店业领导者大部分时间都是通过与酒店客户和外部客户，如供应商、合作伙伴和设计师建立关系等活动与人打交道。他们还须管理和培训团队领导与成员等内部客户。酒店领导经常面临的挑战是人力资源问题，是如何更好地发展与人之间的关系，包括如何培训、再培训和培养人才；如何促使团队合作；如何确保他们热爱工作并拥有共同的信念；如何组织公司并确保和谐有效地运作。

作为首席执行官，我非常关注品牌的愿景和发展轨迹。我努力同与我共事的每一个人培养有意义的关系，并让他们相信自己可以与同事和顾客建立同样的关系。

采访者： 领导与组织文化之间的关系如何？

受访者： 领导者采取的策略对组织文化会产生极大影响，对成功至关重要。一家强大的公司的文化并不局限于拥有和接受某种"信念"，还涉及更深入、更主动的管理方式。举个例子，它涉及从日常简报讨论到员工执行的操作任务的各个方面。我们必须管理公司文化、将其拓展到员工为公司所做的几乎所有工作之中。因此，组织文化是"让我们的员工受到重视，能够与我们共同成长，共同闪耀"。（Faik，2017）

采访者： 什么是关系型领导？关系型领导者对下属的领导是否成功？您认为谁有效实践了关系型领导？

受访者： 关系型领导者无论取得过怎样的成绩，都能谦逊待人。我的祖父和父亲都是成功的领导者，树立了成功的榜样。我的祖父郑裕彤创立了香港最大的房地产公司之一——新世界发展有限公司。他出身草根，尽管缺乏背景优势，但他勤勤恳恳地建立起了自己的商业帝国。几十年来，为新世界集团工作的大批员工对企业表现出了忠诚、信心和对我祖父领导能力的高度敬重。我祖父和我父亲郑家纯是公司内部谦逊待人的典范。他们不仅平易近人，还鼓励员工在快速变化的商业环境中稳步前行。

要想对组织进行持续的改善，领导者必须与他们的团队建立伙伴关系。团队应当兢兢业业，有归属感，为公司做出贡献，对成长的机遇充满信心。世界瞬息万变，瑰丽酒店集团也在不断发展壮大。首席执行官的职责便是不断用新鲜的、创新十足的管理理念和公司理念来推动团队进步。瑰丽不断收集顾客的反馈。顾客具体的体验感受对我们而言是最有价值的，无论体验是积极的还是消极的。这类反馈有助于指导各酒店改进其服务和组织。

采访者： 成功的领导者该如何思考问题？

受访者： 高层领导的决策通常来自其见解和信念。苹果公司的史蒂夫·乔布斯、微软的比尔·盖茨和脸书的马克·扎克伯格等许多成功的高层领导者对产品开发都有着自己独到的见解。他们依据自己的直觉和远见，确定市场需求，并着手开发具有创新性的新产品。他们在研发阶段经历了艰难的开端，在此阶段，他们的决策过程并不依赖研究或事实。如果每项决定都完全依赖研究和事实，我们就永远无法抛开保守和传统的思维方式。

采访者： 您担任公司首席执行官的动机是什么？对公司未来的发展又有何期望呢？

受访者： 我对酒店充满热情，对创建品牌的机遇充满热情，我喜欢新事物、新项目，能够去打造一些你相信能在市场上立足的东西。简而言之，其实热情是驱动力。酒店业领导者是通过寻找新的方式将品牌提升到一个新的层次，从而获得满足感。我毕业于哈佛大学，主修经济学。西方教育和亚洲民族文化的结合帮助我了解了东西方文化。我认为，这为我提供了开阔且具有前瞻性的思维，有助于推动公司向前发展。

我的目标和期望是将瑰丽酒店集团提升至一个新的高度。我希望瑰丽能够成为全球酒店业的领军者，所有人都想来瑰丽工作，并且（酒店集团）不断扩张。在瑰丽雄心勃勃的全球发展和扩张计划背后，是具有远见卓识且平易近人的领导层，他们遵循"关系型酒店"的理念。2018 年，瑰丽宣布了一项发展和扩张计划，计划未来五年内在全球增开 50 家酒店，这对于四家不同酒店品牌的组合来说，扩张规模达到了 70%（Rosentter，2018）。分配每处地产所需的资源是我面临的最大挑战。作为领导者，我必须确保每处地产在质量和经营业绩层面保持一致。这很大程度上取决于雇用并留住合适的人才。我认为这将是整个酒店业最大的问题，因为酒店需要大量的人才来经营。找到并部署合适的人才以保持行业竞争力，这一点非常重要。在此基础上，人力资源管理和雇主品牌化的整个过程对公司至关重要。瑰丽酒店集团有各种计划来支持招聘和选拔流程。雇主品牌计划扩展到学校访问、实习、导师计划和校招。让所有员工知道他们可以在公司内成长和学习，并激励他们在公司内走职业化道路，这一点至关重要，让他们理解和接受公司的愿景和文化也是很重要的。

采访者：领导层中是否存在性别差距？您如何看待女性领导者？

受访者：我主张取消"女性领导者"这一标签。我认为，如果有更多的人采用这种表达，那么刻板印象永远不会改变。性别差异对于领导层来说不是问题，有技术、有能力的领导者也不会受到性别的限制。我认为，自信高于性别。

酒店业是充满活力的"关于人"的业务，其中包含与文化、营销、设计、财务、运营和服务相关的一切事务。在我看来，谦逊、有远见、鼓舞人心、令人信服以及公正是受欢迎的领导风格。

领导酒店教育迈向新高度

受访者： 田桂成教授
职　位： 香港理工大学酒店及旅游业管理学院院长及
讲座教授，郭炳湘基金国际酒店服务业管理教授
采访者： 金博蓝教授

采访者： 您是如何进入酒店和旅游业的？作为酒店教育业的领导者，您前进的动力是什么？

受访者： 第一个问题的答案很简单，因为我一直向往周游世界。我选择酒店和旅游业是因为它可以帮我实现这个梦想。对于第二个问题，我认为主要原因是我有机会改变现状，这也是我不竭的动力源泉。

采访者： 这种动力是向来存在的，还是在您的职业生涯中逐渐发展起来的呢？

受访者： 应该说这种动力已经在许多方面有所改变。我在美国读本科的时候，有一位来自韩国的客座教授，他后来在他的回忆录中提到初次见我的情景，他写道，在美国做客座教授期间听说班里有位韩国学生。留意到我之后，他惊讶于我才到美国不久，虽然还只是个大三的学生，但已经成为学生会主席。该教授参加了由我主持的会议后，他认为我具有较强的领导力。也许成为本领域的领导者是发挥领导潜力的一种途径。也许是我从小天资过人，并且意识到了积极培养领导能力的重要性。

采访者： 下面我们来谈谈酒店和旅游教育领域。有许多普适的领导理论已经在军事、政治或商业等领域得到了应用。但有些领导特质尤其适用于酒店和旅游教育领域。在酒店领域，领导能力有哪些区别于其他领域的特征？您可否分享一下亚洲或其他地区的良好的酒店业领导力范例？

受访者： 各行各业的领导者都应具有一些共同的特点。一是拥有敏锐的判断力或常识。因为生活中很多事情都很简单，所以领导者必须有常识。不幸的

是，很多人似乎缺乏这一点，这阻碍了他们发挥自己成为优秀领导者的潜力。对我来说，常识包括同理心和职业敏感性，还包括文化意识。拥有沟通能力不仅仅局限于语言能力，还关系到与人打交道的方式——沟通方式。领导者要有决心、有魄力做出决定。我认为这是一切领导力的共同特征。但酒店业与旅游业、其他行业有何不同？我们经常与各式各样的利益相关者打交道，这意味着有效的沟通尤为重要。对于工厂的领导者来说，主要任务可能是与员工沟通。在酒店业，许多部门认为他们与经营有着利害关系，设法与他们沟通是至关重要的。此外，我觉得审美技能也是因人而异的。有些人称之为仪容仪表，而有些人称之为"展示技巧"。审美技能需要你具备看到不同事物的能力，例如，更加仔细地看待事物，需要做到既见林又见木。对我而言，这样的能力在酒店和旅游业中尤为重要。微小的东西往往会给顾客带来很大的不同。然而对领导者来说，了解大局也是很重要的。我遇到过一些对大局很在行但对细节视而不见的领导者。另一些人擅长观察小细节，但忽略了大局（他们有时被称作微观管理者）。酒店领导者的重要特质包括敏锐的直觉、多元文化、国际视野和审美能力。领导者应了解微观和宏观环境，并能够评估其对企业的影响。他们应该积极主动、未雨绸缪，以做出有效的应对。

采访者：您提到了教育以及酒店业方面的领导力。您已经概述了酒店业中领导力的典型特征。那么教育领域呢？

受访者：首先，人们应该了解商业环境——它有自己的一套规则。政治技巧也很重要——如何以适当的方式传达你的信息。这取决于受众和具体情况。保持敏感很重要。我在美国工作的时候，人们更喜欢直截了当。然而在亚洲，人们通常不那么直截了当。对于某些事情，你应该直截了当表达自己的观点，而另一些事情就得委婉一些。你得避免引起上级或他人的不安。然后是对他人的情绪保持敏感性。在与相关方接洽后，我们也许可以就有争议的问题私下继续交谈，而不是在其他人面前讨论。这里没有万能公式，你必须自行判断。对我来说，这就是保持敏感性。

采访者：您会将情境领导力作为核心价值吗？

受访者：是的。然而你需要有更宏伟的愿景，有能力进行情境管理且避免使其受损。如果你只管理情境而不维护核心价值，就不会取得任何进展。这就像是设法取悦每个人那样。

采访者：您的经验是如何塑造您的领导风格的呢？它是始终如一的还是在不断发展的呢？

受访者：谈到领导力，总的来说，我觉得大体特征一直保持不变。领导风格反映了一个人的个性和个人经历。就我而言，在历经无数经验和教训后，我学会了更有效地沟通。我从错误中汲取了经验教训。你可以在积累经验和犯错误的过程中学到新的技能。当面对新的情况时，你的反应来自对过去经验的总结。你之前就已经学会了应对新情况的方法。

采访者：有哪位领导者是您特别敬佩的？

受访者：我想以一个人为例，我从他身上学到了很多东西。我以前有位上司非常严厉——我称他为仁慈的独裁者。我说他仁慈是因为他很可敬，富有同情心，并且总试着去理解和沟通。然而他达到目的的决心非常坚定，可以排除一切非议。事实证明他总是对的。即使对某些他已经下定决心的问题，如果遇到阻力，他也总是征求意见。我从他身上学到了"决心"这种领导特质。我刚才提到的上司被贴上了独裁者的标签，因为他会督促工作的进展，同时他尽量做到体恤下属。他部门里的员工能相互沟通、相互商议并达成共识。他也有着优秀的沟通技巧，是那种可以把梳子卖给和尚的人。他很有魅力，是个很好的推销员。他的沟通风格也显示了他的可靠——这种品质总是会大放异彩。我从他那里学会了沟通的艺术。

我还跟随过一位富有创造力的领导。他能够"跳出框架"来思考，并运用自己解决问题的技巧。但他最终不幸遭到了生活和事业的失败，因为缺乏个人诚信和职业操守。我从中得到的教训是，尽管创造力很重要，但诚信才是个人和职业生活的准绳。你可以富有创造力和创新精神，但应该有度。我想象不到哪个人是我想从头到脚都追随的——追随其一举一动。然而，我注意到我所接触的每位领导者都有各自的优点和缺点。我只学习我看重的部分。

采访者：作为酒店及旅游业管理学院院长，除了中国香港、澳门和中国内地的商业环境之外，您还身处高度全球化的外部环境中。您是否有基于中国香港，着眼全球的运营意见？是环境塑造了您的酒店业领导力吗？

受访者：我来到香港后有了一系列全新体验。政治和经济环境与我以前熟悉的大不相同。理解这套新规则，并在其框架下进行运营管理是很有必要的。内地和香港虽然紧邻但有很大不同。你必须了解人际关系以及如何与人沟通、联系。我在内地和香港采用的交流方式截然不同。你需要灵活且随情境而变。

采访者： 在酒店和旅游业中，有大量关于"关系"的文献。您对这一概念在酒店业的应用有什么看法吗？

受访者： 实际上，"关系"概念并不局限于中国内地。它存在于亚洲的许多国家和地区，包括韩国。虽然我已经强调了人际关系对于酒店领导力的重要性，但据我了解，中国的"关系"更加复杂。有些关系本质上是纯粹的金融或经济关系。然而也不能忽视关系本身。也许在 20 多岁的时候，不够完善的人际关系会成为成功的阻碍。根据我在亚洲国家，如泰国、韩国，特别是中国学到的知识，建立融洽的关系、友谊和信任很重要。之后一切就会顺利起来。

采访者： 您提倡"亚洲典范"或者下一波亚洲引领下的浪潮。这关系到亚洲在这场浪潮中扮演的角色。它扮演的角色与欧洲或美国相似吗？这会和以前的浪潮相仿，还是另有特征？

受访者： 理解并表现出对同事、下属和客户的敏感是一个重要的领导特质，在亚洲尤其如此。一些西方管理者往往缺乏这样的敏感性，第一次来到亚洲，西方的领导者往往因此而失败。我以维斯滕酒店的一名总经理为例，讲一下敏感性。他在同一家酒店担任总经理长达 20 余年，堪称传奇人物。他所经营的房地产在各个方面都取得了成功，包括员工满意度和利润方面。之后，新的总经理走马上任，他说："我们可以通过减少员工数量来提高效率。"在某些方面他是对的。但当他开始做出一系列改变时，一些员工很感激，而另一些人则抱怨说希望前任总经理能回来。因此，新的领导者很快就失败了，公司不得不扶持前任总经理上任以稳定局势。该职位随后被移交给另一位经理，而前任总经理被任命为高级副总裁，负责监督新的总经理。这个关于保持敏感性的经典范例说明员工的感受不能简单地用账面数据或财务回报来解释。

采访者： 关于大湾区和全球化我还有一些问题。中国香港正在大湾区寻求机遇。您认为这种不断变化的环境会如何影响我们行业的领导方式？

受访者： 尽管我回答这个问题也许不完全够格，但我观察到许多中国公司正在迅速向海外拓展。它们现在正经历煎熬，因为它们不熟悉其他（非中国）

市场。

采访者： 中国香港是许多顶级酒店公司的亚太总部所在，同时也是一座全球化的都市。全球化的进一步发展是否对酒店业有利？

受访者： 总体上说，尽管酒店公司正在采取各种不同的方法和战略应对全球化，但它是积极的，我们应该接受。以半岛酒店和香格里拉酒店集团为例，尽管官方尚未声明，但半岛集团无疑正在全球化。该公司总部恰恰设在中国香港，但无论产业建在何处都力求提供最好的酒店服务，这就是他们的运营宗旨。虽然香格里拉在很多方面与其相似，但他们更希望被视作亚洲品牌，核心仍是亚洲酒店。这种模式表明他们会提供细致周到的亚洲酒店服务。因此他们希望被视为亚洲品牌，正如曼谷的都喜国际集团希望被看作泰国酒店公司。在宏观或者国家层面，有各种各样的方法来推进这一原则。当日本公司扩张时，他们希望被视为日本公司。丰田公司在泰国的每一位员工都是日本人，客户也可以预计在公司里遇到的都是日本人。然而韩国公司采用了不同的方法。例如，有政策规定，应任命当地（即泰国）的首席执行官来指导其泰国业务。然而，公司会在私下里进行任命——他们很少公开露面或进行演讲。这些方法各不相同，观察这些模式所面临的挑战也很有趣，如丰田的海外扩张。

采访者： 您能提出亚太地区（酒店业）领导者所面临的几项挑战吗？以及下一代（酒店业）领导者，包括现在的酒店专业的大学生未来将面临哪些挑战？

受访者： 中国人和亚洲人的未来是光明的。亚洲公司在海外的扩张速度快于西方公司。我们拥有一批能真正成为全球领导者的人才。语言挑战是未来领导者应该关注的方面。英语已成为商界的通用语言。因此，那些渴望成为全球领导者的中国人或者亚洲人必须精通英语。我认为这对我们的学生来说是一个挑战；要想成为全球领导者就要说一口流利的英语。如果你留意那些最成功的亚洲领导者，他们都会说英语。这是第一个挑战。

另外，必须具有全球和国际意识。请记住，例如，都喜国际集团首席执行官 Suphajee Suthumpun 女士最近为我们的新生做了演讲。当她被调到她雇主（IBM）在纽约的一个管理职位时，在国外，如纽约这样的地方，一位泰国女性担任管理职位并不寻常。然而，她很有能力，对挑战毫不畏惧。许多亚洲人会害怕，有些人甚至有近乎受害者思维。

都喜国际集团董事长 Khun Chanin 就都喜的国际化问题与学生们进行了交谈。该公司派遣了许多泰国员工和领导者到非洲和中东地区工作。许多人想尽快返回泰国，因为他们在本土文化环境中感到更舒适。

Khun Chanin 的无畏使得他和他的家族为员工开启了通向新生活的大门。然而泰国人一般很容易满足，他们寻求幸福的环境。既然如此，为什么还要去寻找新的挑战呢？ Khun Chanin 解释说，很多泰国人喜欢吃猪肉，但是在一些穆斯林国家，猪肉不一定很容易买到。此类事情就是全球化面临的一项挑战。

在中国香港，未来酒店业领导者的调动意愿也是一项挑战。如果你看一下我们的酒店专业学生档案，其中大约 73% 是女性。这在亚洲甚至全球的酒店学校都很常见。尽管对男性、女性都有各自的影响，但想组建家庭的女性还面临着额外的困难。也许是迫于家庭和社会的压力，她们离开家庭，想要在职业上有所发展的难度更大。因此，许多学生更喜欢从事市场营销或人力资源方面的工作，即那些涉及计算机操作和办公室业务的更稳定的岗位。但要知道，公司只有一个副总裁，这是人力资源方面的限制。

采访者： 随着大量高素质人才进入酒店业，行业的思维是否需要随之转变？

受访者： 我认为语言能力与其他技能是并驾齐驱的。考虑一下思考问题的态度。良好的语言技能伴随着自信出现。如果我英语有缺陷，让你难以理解，自信会使我把这看作对你的一种考验，而不是我自身的问题。自信有助于弥补某些不足。

采访者： 下一代领导者是否面临语言之外的挑战？我指的是数字技术颠覆性地改变了产业结构，人们对节能也有了更高期望。这些问题可能需要重新思考。之前的领导者是否从未考虑过这些问题？

受访者： 对我来说，出生于 20 世纪八九十年代的新一代人本身才是最大的挑战。亚洲的新一代人生活条件优渥，以至于满足到缺乏努力的动力。当我们将其与那些希望证明自己，并更积极地追求事业的前辈们所面临的情况进行比较时，会发现这是一个巨大的挑战。新一代太娇惯了。例如在中国香港，当我早上从健身房回来的时候，经常能看到有些孩子在上学路上拿着智能手机听音乐，旁边有女佣帮他背书包。有时女佣比学生还矮小，但还要背书包。我觉得这颇具象征性。新一代人被照顾得太好了，我都不知道他们靠自己能做些什么。如果是六七岁的孩子，我可以理解；但是十几岁的少年为什么要女佣背书包？我想他们在家里也不会自己铺床。作为领导者，他们又能做些什么呢？我很担忧。

采访者： 您鼓励我们学校的学生要独立和有责任感，也分享了自己在就读酒店学校时学习从事手工工作（如切胡萝卜）的价值。还鼓励中国香港的学生洗碗，这是了解酒店基本功能的一部分。

受访者： 香港学生在家不洗碗，所以他们会想为什么在学校要这么做？我认为欧洲或者美国的酒店学校不会雇人替学生洗碗。这是一种世代相传的文化。

采访者： 您对即将接班的年轻领导者以及行业如何对待新一代人有什么看法吗？

受访者： 我认为我们需要师徒制度，不管是正式还是非正式的项目。这是培养接班人的有效方法。每一位领导者都必须扮演下一代人的导师，帮助他们为未来领导过程中的挑战做好准备。在酒店及旅游业管理学院，我们安排了教授为低年级学生提供指导，还有让学生跟从行业导师的计划。

采访者： 在这方面，行业总体的进展顺利吗？

受访者： 我认为个人或组织的领导力导师差异很大。有时，指派的导师忙于日常工作，忙于完成每月甚至每天的目标。良好的实践需要建立一定的培养流程，并形成能培育领导者和领导力的文化。我们学校已在积极地践行这些措施。

采访者： 香港理工大学酒店及旅游业管理学院有着辉煌的成绩，在访谈最后您能和大家分享一下领导学校的心得吗？

受访者： 我的领导风格和哲学受到我的宗教信仰和《圣经》中的领导理念的影响。《圣经》有66卷，里面每一个词最终都指向"爱"。传达出上帝爱他的子民，派圣子牺牲自己来拯救生灵。所以《圣经》的本质就是爱，这就是我个人价值观的来源。另外，成长的文化环境塑造了我的性格。由于我在韩国度过了青年时期，所以我的交流方式明显受到了韩国文化的影响。还有，我在美国所受的高等教育影响了我对西方世界的理解，并延伸到了工作和生活中。这种西方和亚洲兼备的思维方式对我在中国香港的工作很有帮助。

我的领导风格对于我们的学校发展到今天是很重要的。一方面，我总是和我的同事分享荣誉。不管愿景多小，我的同事总愿为其出力。另一方面，我和其他人一起为他们的愿景加油打气，这样他们就会有动力坚持下去。每个人都有参与感，即使只在摇旗呐喊也行。领导者一个人不能做所有事，而支持者有助于创造愿景。我记得当我刚来到这里的时候，我独自想出了校训。校训大意是引领亚洲的酒店和旅游业。起初，很多人嘲笑、挖苦我，他们问我怎么会大言不惭地说这所学校要引领亚洲。然而几年后，人们开始说我是对的，有人建议我们用更有力的表达——我们不仅引领教育领域，而且引领着酒店和旅游业。现在，我们强势踏入了新的领域。我相信，如果你有愿景，能与他人交流，为每个人加油鼓劲，你的同事都会乐意接纳你。我认为这些就是领导的重要特质。

冉冉升起的女性领袖创新观点

受访者： 邱咏筠女士，太平绅士
职　位： 帝盛酒店总裁兼执行董事
采访者： 金博蓝教授

受访者： 酒店业对我而言，一直以来都是以非常个人化的方式与我交流。由于我的一部分家族生意是拥有和经营酒店，我很幸运从小就接触到这个行业。特别是 20 多年前，第一次在香港丽思卡尔顿酒店的实习经历给我留下了深刻印象。当时，该酒店是最具创新精神的高端酒店品牌之一，每一位全球员工都要牢记"丽思卡尔顿信条"——"我们是女士与绅士，为女士与绅士服务"。还有"服务三部曲"以及"十二条服务价值观"，放在自己的衣兜里。其中包括简单而重要的服务标准与核心价值观，必须铭记于心，包括称呼客人的名字，并且时刻关注、预测每位客人的需求。这证明：个性化、人性化的服务对酒店品牌的成功非常重要，时至今日仍然适用。酒店业可能在不断发展，但当今最大的消费趋势是全球化以及更高、更复杂的定制化需求。

采访者： 您的家人支持您在酒店行业实习吗？

受访者： 我很庆幸有父母的支持，无论我选择了什么，他们都支持我。我做过很多实习工作，其中有一次是工程类实习，也有一段时间在银行和零售业工作。我很快就意识到：对我而言，最重要的是能够为各行各业的人提供平台，让他们在这个平台上努力工作、成长与进步。服务业的"准入门槛"较低，不一定需要受过高等教育就能出类拔萃或发展事业，这一点对我很有启发。通过创造一种公司文化，使员工得到激励、授权和培养，我自然而然地在为客人提供服务的同时，也会给他们倾注同样的体贴和关怀。

采访者： 您现在还很年轻，是什么让您坚持在这个领域继续发展？

受访者： 酒店业时刻有新事物产生，无论是在不同地方创立企业，还是扩展产品的种类。由于最终目的是为了满足消费者的需求，我们必须时刻关注消费者的喜好。我们（帝盛酒店）既是业主，也是运营商，这使我们有机会为物业增值，即使当时的房地产或物业市场充满着挑战。我们在选择购买物业时非常注重策略，确保购买的物业不仅物有所值，而且该地区的旅游有足够的增长潜力。我喜欢把我们的每家酒店都看作所在城市的形象大使，这使我们的酒店始终保持它令人振奋的状态。帝盛酒店品牌承诺是"活力四射"，反映了酒店在 27 个城市中的每个城市，如何拥抱社区和周边环境，为我们的客人提供当地特色艺术、文化和时尚体验。

采访者：您如何看待酒店服务？

受访者：酒店服务包括的不仅仅是酒店。一切都归结为服务，只有最优秀的人才能做到这一点，即那些充满热情的员工，他们希望看到客人走出酒店时的微笑比入住时更开心。这是所有领导者和经理应该在内部培养的东西，这将自然地反映在员工对待客人的方式上。然而，仅靠服务本身还不够。消费者需要的不仅仅是最好的价值，更需要能与他们亲身交流与互动的体验。作为酒店服务的领导者，你需要时时关注这些细微差别，利用好不同的渠道。

例如，我们全新改版后的网站会根据访客的地理位置，自动为访客定制最佳体验。考虑到中国内地游客使用的平台不同，我们的网站用开放街景地图取代了谷歌地图，并以微信等内地游客熟悉的渠道显示，而不用 Instagram 或 Facebook。我们也是最早开通微信支付渠道的酒店集团之一。

在过去，为每间客房安上最新型号的电视可能是一种奢侈；而现在，这被认为是酒店基本服务的一部分，同时好的床和淋浴设备也是必需。咖啡机、高速无线网络以及 USB 接口亦是如此。一切都在日新月异，这也包括客人对酒店基本住宿设施的期望。我们是最早在每间客房内提供免费数据电话的酒店之一，这样客人可以随时与外界保持联系。现在，我们通过与 Foodpanda 合作，向客人开放了食物配送服务，让客人可以轻松地从最好的餐厅点餐并直接送到房间。如果没有领导层的开放和超前于这种变化，我们就很难跟上时代。

此外，我们还计划推出"帝盛发现（Dorsett Discoveries）"——通过精心策划的活动与合作伙伴关系，为宾客提供丰富的体验，介绍酒店所在城市的"好吃、好玩、好乐"的地方。我们将与艺博展和索尼世界摄影大奖合作，超越通常的四星级体验，将酒店客人与国际最新的艺术文化联系在一起，同时吸引那些对艺术和当地城市充满热情的人来我们酒店。

我觉得我真正培养了一个开放与合作的领导环境，让我们的管理团队无论职位或头衔，都能够互相学习，也向员工学习。最近，我们帝盛酒店所有当地酒店团队完成了一次全球品牌建设活动，不同部门走到一起，集思广益，大家提出一些新举措和营销理念，能够代表我们品牌以及我们希望成为的品牌。这不仅能使我们的团队更深入地参与其中，让他们更加主动，同时也是很好的工具，从每天在一线服务客人的员工那里获得反馈和了解情况。这种包容以及愿意和享受待客服务、奉献精神和超前思维能力，正是我希望团队具备的领导素质。

采访者： 您的酒店业领导者榜样是谁？

受访者： 显然有很多榜样。我不会特指某个个体，因为术业有专攻。话虽如此，令我印象特别深刻的是：万豪在收购喜达屋之后，很快就将所有的新资源整合在一起，不仅为客人提供更多的酒店服务，而且还进行了创新式技术提升，如通过他们的应用程序提供移动和无钥匙入住服务，并在客人到达前 24 小时内与酒店管理人员进行实时聊天。万豪的轻资产模式使其能够吸引新的业主加入到其各个品牌中来，并在创新销售与营销方面投入更多的资金，实现了迅速扩张。此外，瑰丽酒店专注于设计与创新，其独特之处在于打造强大、现代和差异化的品牌。瑰丽酒店相信：真正的款待服务来自与同事、客人、合作伙伴及社区建立起牢固持久的关系。

我相信帝盛酒店的垂直整合模式能够以更全面、更可持续的方式扩大我们的规模。因此，我们能够灵活优化每个市场的定价和收入，更快速地调整和个性化我们的产品，并更好地控制产品与服务质量。我们与战略合作伙伴合作，如在日本和欧洲拥有系列酒店的 Agora 酒店集团与 Transworld 酒店集团，我们能够利用集体资源，并利用这些专业知识继续在新地区进行扩张。与万豪邦威一样，我们最近推出的会员计划"帝盛礼赏"也使客人可以在不同品牌的酒店中累计积分并兑换优惠。不过，我们更进一步，提供"部分现金，部分积分"的模式，让会员无论累计了多少积分，都可以随时兑换奖励。

采访者： 考虑到帝盛经营的大环境，贵酒店公司总部位于中国香港的事实对您的行业领导地位有何影响？

受访者： 中国香港商业大环境下的竞争很激烈。单是香港房地产成本，就令经营酒店的成本高昂，更不用说拥有酒店了。这迫使我们在精打细算每平方米的价格时，必须更加严格，这也是我们在所有市场上要定期监测的。当然，作为酒店从业者，我也关注服务，但也必须实事求是。如果一个物业建设被设计成写字楼，可能会带来更好的商业回报。这也是拥有自己资产无疑带来优势的地方。

由于整体商业环境竞争激烈，香港人的效率往往很高。即使香港的员工与客房比例相对较低，但是我们在服务上并未打折扣。虽然我们在过去两年遇到了挑战（由于2015—2017年香港旅游业出现了下滑），但我们的业务表现仍然优于市场，入住率为86%~90%，近期我们的业务表现非常好，入住率为90%~95%。

每个地区的经营环境都有其独特之处。比如日本，那里的风格分等级，餐饮的重要性和成本支出更多，毛利润较低。

采访者：您如何看待商业中的"关系"？

受访者：无论是在日本还是在英国，生意中你要做的很多事情就是处理关系，即多年来建立和投资的人脉关系。随着世界变得越来越全球化，现在人人都有关系。不同的是，选择合作对象与合作伙伴时要慎重、尊重和真诚，确保你的生意或品牌理念有协同效应和共同目标。即使是在中国内地，商业世界也越来越透明。因此，与合适的人保持一致非常关键。

采访者：在中国内地开展业务的经营理念是什么？

受访者：我们的业务主要集中在中国内地市场，我们在中国内地的几家酒店分别位于上海、武汉、成都和沿海城市。由于我们在中国香港有很多物业，所以策略与运营重点放在与中国香港有相似之处的内地城市。由于我们在中国香港的运营经验已经很成熟，所以当内地消费者开始出国旅游的时候，我们是最早接触到内地消费者的酒店之一。这些游客的第一目的地往往是中国香港。以前的情况肯定是这样，内地游客在出国前一定会先到这里来，然后再出国。所以，我们对内地游客的喜好非常了解。

例如，我们在世界各地的酒店都可以使用微信支付。我们在内地游客最初预订的时候就使他们感到方便。我们在全球范围内的所有酒店，包括欧洲的酒店，都会提供全套的中式早餐。我们在亚洲各地的四星级酒店，包括在内地，秉持提供全系列便利设施的理念。不过，我发现在伦敦的四星级酒店不一定能提供所有这些服务。这使我们可以把所有酒店中了解到的客户行为和需求落实到各个酒店中去，这也是我们进行客人情况统计要继续的工作。

采访者： 根据您在英国的考察结果，您能详细阐述一下这种不同的经营方式吗？专注于中国内地市场，然后外包出去？

受访者： 对中国内地消费者而言科技很重要，而且技术和电商平台也在激增。内地在这方面比香港要先进，甚至比世界的其他国家还要先进。现在我们在与电商平台合作，如果顾客在这样的平台上进行购买，他们可以选择在酒店收货，也可以直接送货到房间。有些境外物品无法直接递送到内地，于是内地客人可以要求电商把物品发到香港的酒店，自己取到后再带回内地。中国人也渴求知识。像你注意到的，有些度假村会提供某种迎宾饮料。我们会提供以品牌冠名的帝盛葡萄酒，顾客可以享用免费饮料。不只是把客人聚到一起，我们还会介绍不同的话题以供讨论。例如，最近一个话题是关于当代艺术，一些来自香港艺术学校的艺术家们亲临现场进行了阐述和讲解。客人有很大的求知欲。你介绍周围地区的文物精华，他们也很感兴趣。

采访者： 您认为大中华区酒店服务领导者面临的主要挑战是什么？

受访者： 我一直认为发掘人才是件很有挑战性的事情，尤其是在内地的二三线城市，那里酒店如雨后春笋一样迅速发展起来。虽然它们可能进入城市的时间有点早，但我觉得这种情况很快就会自我修正。还有更多在海外工作的中国人开始回国发展或通过国际集团回国，带回了更多的经验。

我对集团要求的最重要原则就是城市核心策略，不管是大中华区还是全球。这是因为城市会变得越来越重要。人们将继续频繁前往中国香港、日本东京、英国伦敦和美国纽约等地，因为这些城市也是通往附近目的地的枢纽。即使在城市类别中，也有很多不同的机会。由于英国国内旅游的人数在不断增加，我们计划在伦敦提供一个新的服务式公寓类别。我目前的重点是在英国、日本扩张，并在未来几年内进入澳大利亚。

采访者： 未来酒店领导面临的挑战是什么？

受访者： 考虑到下一代时，我想到了我的子女和侄女、侄子。他们在网络和社交媒体中的交流方式不尽相同，这对他们很重要。未来酒店的目的可能会变得非常不同。假日宾馆可能在 20 年前就已经流行起来，但目前的趋势已经转向共享资源。年轻人对共享房间、共享平台、共享工作空间的想法是相当开放的。都是与某一个品牌联系在一起，因为这个品牌与自己的生活方式或理念相吻合。我最近去了阿姆斯特丹的几家五星级酒店，很多都是自助服务。我可以理解为什么很多千禧一代人喜欢在自己的时间内灵活点餐和付款。这就是为什么我们与 Foodpanda 合作，在客房内整合了精心设计的菜单，让客人拥有同样的独立性和灵活性。

采访者： 在像我们这样的酒店院校，大约 70% 的学生是女性。在中国香港，这些学生会遇到很多年纪较大的西方男性经营和管理的酒店。我们的下一代人，尤其是女学生，学习酒店专业前景如何？您认为行业中有障碍吗？

受访者： 根据 *Women Hospitality* 创始人 Julia Campbell 的说法，2017 年酒店业中女性的比例为 55.5%，然而大部分管理职位仍由男性担任。然而，我们帝盛的领导团队和酒店管理层中大部分都是由女性组成的。在酒店中肯定需要更多的性别平衡，而且我觉得作为一名女总裁，我不仅能更多地考虑到客人的需求，也能更多地考虑到同事，无论是男性还是女性的需求。如果同事说她得去参加儿子的学校招生面试，我会立刻批准她去。甚至我的男同事也会向我表达这些需求。虽然在领导岗位和工作场所中的平等代表权都非常重要，但我认为这也是为公司创造包容、宽容和培养的环境。这就是承认个人成长所需的需求与平衡。

我相信这要归结于业务性质和我们培养的文化。纵观我们的酒店，大部分总经理都有销售和营销背景。很多其他酒店的总经理都是从餐饮业背景走出来的，这往往意味着更多的男性。我们业务的一大重点是销售和营销。

采访者： 对于毕业生中很少有人选择长期留在餐饮业的现象，您感到惊讶吗？我感觉到他们希望行业领导者对于如何成为龙头企业可以保持开放的心态，而且他们不一定希望通过传统的道路到达领导岗位。

受访者： 我觉得这一点都不奇怪。公司的招聘方式正在发生变化，尤其是酒店业。你不一定非得上过酒店管理学院才会成功；来自不同背景而志同道合的人聚集在一起工作，他们各自带来了新想法和知识，可以帮助公司继续前进。找到一个人的激情，并将其与工作内容相结合，意味着可以从他们那里得到更多，因为你既满足了他们的兴趣，又满足了公司的利益。归根结底，酒店服务工作就是要提供令人难忘的体验，并建立起真正的人际关系——如果不投资培养合适的人，就无法做到这一点。

粤港澳大湾区内外酒店业领导力

受访者： 何超琼女士
职　位： 信德集团有限公司集团行政主席兼总经理
采访者： 金博蓝教授

采访者： 您进入酒店行业的契机是什么？

受访者： 我进入这个行业是出于一些机缘巧合。我在参与家族业务（信德集团）后，先是从自己干企业传播和营销业务做起。信德集团是我父亲在澳门经营各项综合业务时创立的旗舰企业，涉及酒店、房地产和物流。在我自己做公关和企业传播的时候，也曾接触过酒店业和旅游业客户。

大约 20 年前，在澳门国际机场的开发项目中，需要有人协助提出企业营销建议。我父亲说，当时澳门没有十分符合资格的代理机构，所以计划找一家总部设在中国香港的公司。最初预计会请"四大会计师事务所"之一参与，但后来出于对预算的综合考虑而作罢，更重要的是，那时担心事务所对澳门的定位缺乏真正的了解。在小小的澳门建设一个庞大的国际机场是项宏伟的愿景，这个项目需要一个理解中国香港和澳门关系的人。

在一次轻松的家庭聚餐时聊起这件事，我说："让我来做吧，我很想参与。"初次进军澳门成功后，我继续担任机场公司的独立顾问，而不是担任行政高管职务。后来父亲说："大家都觉得你干得不错。"到了后期阶段，机场公司对人们的需求有了更多了解，也意识到除了提供公共交通服务之外，其他服务也有进一步改善的余地。除了提升整体目的地形象之外，还需要有更多针对市场和客户的业务。由于他们在建设机场，因此增加额外服务也许会扩大网络效应，但他们却不了解如何与香港国际机场竞争或相辅相成。如何吸引中国和亚洲各地的运输公司考虑使用澳门机场。通过规模相对较小的调查和定位研究，他们意识到需要更多相关领域的专业人士。由于我父亲的投资公司是主要的利益相关者和合作伙伴，他想："也许你应该加入这家公司，而不仅仅是作为独立顾问参与。"自此，我开始在更大的领域进行发展。如今我已经在旅游与酒店业领域积累了近30年的经验。

参与机场业务后，我开始在澳门一家航空公司担任董事。在这种关系的基础上，澳门特别行政区政府旅游局参与其中，并在澳门回归祖国前夕帮助塑造了该市的旅游业规模。如果澳门要充分发挥其潜力，就需要开展一系列营销和重新定位活动。我父亲告诉了我澳门特别行政区当时的情况。那时候，澳门特别行政区旅游局并没有直接经营各处国际代表机构，而是由他们独自管理，而且当时只有我父亲经营博彩租界。澳门需要一个过渡期，将各国际代表机构移交给特别行政区政府新成立的澳门特别行政区政府旅游局。我受指派在将近两年的时间里协助完成过渡工作。在此期间，我与前任旅游局董事密切合作，并作为合伙人密切配合旅游局开展工作。

我们共同努力，转移了一些外展办事处，进行会谈并建立了一些新的机构。通过这次项目，我学到了很多东西，并直接参与了旅游与酒店业的市场营销、营运规划和策略管理。虽然我对这个行业一直有兴趣也有信心，但那次巧合才是契机。我从未把旅游与酒店业看作只关乎商业收益和回报的纯商业行为。从一开始我就很了解这个行业的重要性以及如此重要的原因，毕竟澳门高度依赖打造旅游型经济，这一过渡显然是为了澳门未来的发展。

采访者：我们也采访过一些从其他领域进入旅游业与酒店业的内地高管。那么您是如何从传播行业向大公司领导转型的呢？

受访者：我最初的主要工作是开拓愿景和使命以确保基础设施的建设。这就涉及为各行业利益相关者展示明确的未来道路。

当我后来从商时，我越来越重视其他各相关方的角色，因为他们是基础设施的最终使用者。同样，我也以自己作为参与者的身份去理解一些需求和意愿。我们需要确保这不仅是一个想法，还要得到实际的执行。我们需要把好的想法付诸实践，利用它们创造价值，得到商业回报。在过渡期间，我参与了规划和实施的工作。我被正式邀请并担任工程师，重组经营港澳轮渡业务的"信标"合作企业。我负责整个项目，需要着眼于我们的近期项目运作需求，并从旅游经济的宏观角度来纵览全局。我们该如何让企业在不断变化的环境中生存？我很快意识到，情况比我想象的要复杂得多。我应该重点关注基本的商业原则，即成本管理和人力资源，并评估未来的前景。因此，我精心策划了接下来的重新营运事宜。

接下来是一系列重大的并购活动，涉及将我们的部分业务与一些竞争对手的业务合并。一个更强大的团队应运而生，最终消除了重复和竞争。通过这一进程，我们对供需情况进行了严肃评估，预计了一些外部因素，包括影响业务的相关因素。你可以想象，各种与成本相关的问题最终会回到一个问题——如何与我们的供应商及客户合作。我们需要对整个业务策略进行全面复查。通过这次的业务营运经验，我从买卖双方的角度看待行业资产。这不仅仅是先建立一些机构，然后把活动卖给潜在的买家，而是必须每天 24 小时待命，不断与客户及整个行业保持联系。对我来说，一个重要的收获是了解到，旅游与酒店业是一个包含多元化的行业，有许多独一无二的特点。如果只是坐在办公室里做高层决定或者看资产负债表，那永远不会成功。我们需要参与各项业务的各个层面。

我们最初遇到了各种劳工问题，这些问题是由两家有着不同组织文化的公司合并所致。从一开始，员工就对自己的工作保障和职业前景感到不安。甚至在合同尚未签署时，就有罢工事件发生。于是我们必须刻不容缓地处理各种人力资源问题。这让我意识到，在运营某个部门或企业，或是与其共事时，必须了解它的所有方面。这绝不只是做高层工作，而是必须时刻准备好卷起衣袖，亲自上阵干活。你需要解决各种各样的问题。

采访者：无论是酒店与旅游业还是其他领域的领导者，这些人身上是否有您特别欣赏的领导特质？在国内或者全球范围内，您是否有榜样人物或者是学习的目标？

受访者：从我接触同行和行业领袖的经验来看，他们都有一个共同点，特别是在旅游与酒店业，他们将所从事的行业视为毕生的事业。我也接触过许多不同的行业，因为信德公司的业务组合也涉及其他领域的投资，比如房地产的投资和开发。在处理这些领域时，我们必须积累一定的专业知识。房地产行业的原则之一是，一个项目建成并售出之后，就需要"向前看"。不管你对这一成就有多自豪。

也许你凭借在当地积累的专业知识和经验教训，已经将经营范围扩大到海外。但最初的开发成就已经过去，无论是现存的建筑，还是简历里的辉煌，都是如此。你必须定期重新审视你的初衷，并进行升级或者改进。这样能让你重新关注某个特定的项目。旅游与酒店业始终是全天候工作。即使你已经拥有超过 500 家酒店的投资经历，你也永远不能停止与时俱进。为了满足当前和不断发展的标准，你需要不断提升服务质量。这是由客户决定的，而不是你。客户的需求在不断发展进步，你也需要不断升级自身来迎合需求。你不能说："没关系，这些都是比较旧的酒店，我不需要担心，我只需要关注新的领域和项目。"

你所做的一切工作都应该是一致且严密的，否则最终会自食其果。我所见到的众多不同领袖总会时时评估他们自身与当前市场趋势和实践的相关性。这赋予了旅游与酒店业人士独特和创新的性格。现在人人都谈创新，好像它本身是什么新东西一样。但创新其实一直都在。在酒店业，创新必须时刻进行一刻不休，否则成功将难以维系。

采访者： 您认为粤港澳大湾区对酒店业的影响是什么？

受访者： 自从针对粤港澳大湾区的国家政策颁布以来，这一主题引起了大家的高度关注。我们现在认识到，此事迫在眉睫、势在必行。所有的基础设施已经布局完毕。就我而言，我们很幸运，因为我们参与并提供了一部分重要的公共交通设施。由于公司在持续向前推进及扩大规模，我们需要了解和学习珠江三角洲城市和地区内的关系会如何发展。这项工作我们从十几年前就开始了，从那时开始我们就在思考业务应该走向何方。

我们是最先知道港珠澳大桥开发潜力的人。幸运的是，在政府参与之前，我参加了最早的讨论过程。我组建了一个委员会，最初是由私营部门而不是公共部门支持的。我父亲参加了早期的论坛讨论，倡导和分析了建桥的可行性。

我还记得自己参加过一个早期的会议。有人告诉我："超琼，一旦大桥建成，你的轮渡生意就会结束，没有生意。"我说："所以我在这里就更重要了。我既不是敌人也不是间谍。我只是需要学习，也许你日后也会需要我的帮助，利用我的数据和经验来帮助你弄清楚自己需要了解的知识。你需要这些知识才能构思桥梁设计。"所以，我很幸运。在过去的十年里，信德覆盖了更多目的地和线路，不仅是香港与澳门之间，还横跨了整个珠江三角洲。我们也在第一线加深了对其他地方的了解，而不仅仅是在地理或旅行距离方面。我们开始与这些城市的人们合作，也因此了解了他们对未来的想法和愿景——他们想成为什么，以及他们如何看待他们在珠江三角洲建设项目中的目标——我们现在称珠江三角洲为粤港澳大湾区。

虽然粤港澳大湾区作为地区的面积相对较小，但在许多方面都非常博大。尽管我们都说同样的方言（粤语），但对于彼此的差异性和相似性的理解仍然非常有限。尽管文化上有许多共同之处，但除了香港与深圳、澳门与珠海之间的直接关系之外，几乎没有什么直接联系。如果我们讨论的是同化所有人，那么不同的思维方式之间还有相当大的距离。这可以进一步延伸到对强项和弱项的看法，以及谁应该做些什么。我们很早就意识到，这项任务需要一个以具体措施为基础的博弈计划。现在，在国家政府的帮助下，粤港澳大湾区在基础设施发展和这一概念的运作方面有了明确的政策指示。我相信，各个相关城市的发展将逐步使我们各方都能找到自己的优势，从而共同合作。

对我们各方来说，局限于一些非常具体的事情，从而变得高度专业化是不切实际的。显然，有些地区不能专门从事新领域，因为它们长期以来有着各自成熟的经济发展。专业化不能简单地通过设计实现，各方都需要以舒适的方式互相合作。出现重叠是不可避免的。比方说，你不能指定只有深圳才能发展以技术为基础的大产业，而其他地区则不能。事实上，竞争的空间必须存在，这才符合开放市场的理念。在考虑如何在现有优势的基础上继续发展时，我们应该如何利用每个地区的既有事物？我们应该充分利用这一点，再汇集我们的各种多样化资源。例如，就澳门而言，我们的目标是要有竞争力，即使这意味着需要与香港等地竞争。

人力是当前需要关注的问题。尽管澳门目前的就业情况已达到饱和，但对于发展会展行业仍有很强的积极性。我们都知道，香港在这一领域中长期是整个亚洲的领导者。我们现在需要共同努力促进增长，7000 万人口将为我们创造条件。粤港澳大湾区所在的广东省拥有 1 亿居民，而其经济容量已经占中国经济总容量的三分之一。有粤港澳大湾区作为大本营，国际企业有很大的空间来利用这一独特的机会。会展业在香港和澳门已经颇具规模，珠海（横琴岛）

也在不断发展会展业。我们不应该只是互相竞争，抢占现有市场，而应该共同努力，扩大覆盖范围。区域一体化是一个令人感兴趣的挑战，越来越多的新合作途径将会涌现。我预计粤港澳大湾区将建立一个会展组织网络，将所有与会展相关的营运商聚集在一起。针对旅游业专业知识以及资源共享的问题，我们应该进行真诚的讨论。我们一直在说，大桥建成后，生活会变得更好，因为所有的元素都会更接近。每个想去澳门的人都可以在许多新酒店中进行挑选。同样，我们也应该鼓励香港继续开发新的酒店。在我看来，有何不可呢？

每当我遇到海外商务客人时，他们都会分享关于是否会向中国各个地区拓展的决策。当我问他们是否去过中国澳门时，他们通常会说没有。我就会劝他们亲自去看看。尽管他们有时担心自己的企业可能并不适合澳门的环境，但这并不是关键。他们只有真正看到了澳门，以及横琴岛和广东省其他地区的多样性，才能判断他们的企业是否适合这里。我们对香港的业务持不同看法，因为大家都知道，这是初来者的第一站。他们会不断涌来，且永远不会放弃香港。例如，就像去意大利旅行一样，我们几乎总会想要在米兰停留——去购物或参观艺术画廊。这些地方是重要的枢纽城市——主要的城市中心。但你也会想去看看其他地方，拓展对整个国家的了解。这就是我们一直在粤港澳大湾区做的事情。这里有广州和香港；有旅游区，比如澳门，将来还可能会有横琴。所有这些前瞻性的发展都涉及帮助游客了解粤港澳大湾区的意义、接待能力和前景。

重要的不仅仅是香港和澳门。我们国家也将继续作为一个整体发展，这也将继续为我们创造更多机会。

采访者：如何看待粤港澳大湾区未来 20 年有远见的变革型领导力？

受访者：就我个人过去的经历而言，我从未停止过了解我们国家的决策和发展以及中国政府对中国的能力和全球定位的看法。我也很了解中国政府与其他国家的关系和外交的必要性。有人会问："你为什么变得如此关心政治？"但这不仅仅是政治层面，更关乎拥有全球视角和愿景。我们需要明白，我们在香港取得商业发展很容易，因为一切似乎都是商业驱动的。为什么？尽管我们现在正在努力利用新出现的机会，但我们甚至不了解自己，也不知道该如何克服一些被凸显的所谓分歧。当外国运营商或投资者想与我们一起工作时，我们该怎么办？对我们来说，以领导人的身份给予鼓励也许非常重要。

我们应该继续借助中国香港和澳门人民所表现出的特殊能量。我们已经有了与海外企业和人员合作的丰富知识和经验。我们也应该对自己的国家有更多的了解，这样我们才能成为一座桥梁。我们在企业方面做得也很出色。当外人可以直接进入这一区域的不同地区时，这里将会加快开放的脚步，也许当地和国际发展也会有类似的步伐。我们是否应该把主动采取行动称为一种特殊的能力？也许这也是领导力的一种。

采访者：您谈到了海外公司在粤港澳大湾区的机会。我们香港理工大学大部分酒店管理专业的学生都会说粤语、普通话和英语。根据您对下一阶段发展的看法，您觉得说汉语的酒店管理专业学生在思考时，该如何超越中国香港和澳门来拓宽视野？

受访者：18 年前，当澳门特别行政区政府想开放澳门时，永利酒店和威尼斯人酒店来了。以这种方式开放时，很显然，你需要吸引该领域最好的人才，而不是将机会局限于那些已经在亚洲具有影响力的公司，当然包括我父亲的公司。这就是重点，经过 50 年的营运，你需要世界上最优秀的专业人士来提供不同视角。这并不是说澳门企业做得不好，但确实需要吸引新的注意力来达到更高的水平。这不是比较、批评，也不是在提倡外国思想更好或更优越。最终，他们可能也需要调整业务。他们必须明白，他们正在努力建设一种不同的市场，这是世界上最大的市场。以复星集团为例，这家公司并不是以娱乐业或旅游业起家，却完成了一项具有代表性的投资案例。他们购买了太阳马戏团在中国的版权，并将为此在杭州建立一个综合景区，包括主题公园、酒店、培训、学校等。

这并不是说我们从来没有创办马戏团的能力。几年前，我访问了太阳马戏团，因为他们说自己是拉斯维加斯最大的此类演出提供商，美高梅度假酒店仍然是他们的独家合作伙伴。所以我们一直与他们保持联系，就合作前景交换意见，无论是在澳门还是与复星集团合作。其中，我们就中国其他地区的一项具体工作展开了一些讨论。当我去蒙特利尔拜访他们的时候，我发现 30% 的员工是中国人。他们打算带着他们的创意返回中国。他们已经在其他市场有很大影响力，并且积累了多年的经验，他们将把这些资产都带到中国。首先，这将为我们自己的本土表演提供一个新的视角，可以了解他们如何将技巧动作变成娱乐表演。我可以预见，这对双方的未来都将大有益处。今后，我们将看到新一代的伙伴关系和合作，共同发展新的旅游和娱乐理念。我坚信，这一天一定会到来，而且将会产生巨大的影响力。这就是创新的意义所在——集思广益。不再是仅仅让一方采纳另一方的想法，也不是强迫两方互相让步，而是开创一场全新的创意潮流。

我相信这是可以实现的，某种意义上，这也是我通过与美高梅的合作在澳门所做的事情。在建设房产时，我们永远不会采用"拉斯维加斯式"的概念。首先，我们每个人的目标都是表现出对行业要求的理解。然后我们试图创造一些全新的、刺激的东西。只有通过这种方法，我们才能持续地吸引客户。每年出境游的游客数量已经达到了 1.2 亿。如果只提供拉斯维加斯式的体验，那他们没有理由留在这里。明明可以去拉斯维加斯，为什么要来澳门呢？我认为，今后针对我国 14 亿人口的竞争是十分激烈的。这里也许是世界上最适合用来试验旅游与酒店业新营销理念的地方。

采访者：您个人的领导风格是什么？

受访者：我喜欢引导和帮助身边的人，鼓励他们朝着一个目标努力。说到底，不仅是我的所言所思。我希望人们知道，我是来帮忙的，也是来贡献我的团队能够提供的知识的。我与他人分享我的见解和我可以动用的力量。我自己也会做很多调查研究，我可以用亲身经历告诉人们，一切最终都归结于准备工作——调查研究。虽然你可以永远听别人说话，但他们的结论还是根据他们自己的观点得出的。大家都知道伟大的思想家可以提出十分有趣的观点。不过，我真诚地认为，所有这些伟大的思想家在得出结论之前都要做大量的准备工作！

采访者：那么，您会让其他同事拥有更多自主权吗？

受访者：是的。我要求每一个相关的人都要完成同样的工作量。我们分享不同的观点。有时我可能更有资格提出批评和意见，并解释为什么某个看法是准确或者不准确的。不过，归根结底，我的工作就是去协助所有的合作对象，让大家互相理解从而达成共识。

成为酒店业与娱乐相结合的"超级产业"

受访者：吕耀东先生
职　位：银河娱乐集团副主席
采访者：金博蓝教授

采访者：是什么促使您投身酒店和博彩业的?

受访者：我父亲称得上是中国香港成功人士的范例之一。在第二次世界大战时，他从中国内地来到中国香港。他没有受过教育，所以只能白手起家。因缘巧合下，（20世纪50年代末和20世纪60年代初）他结识了一些从事建筑行业的朋友。当时，中国香港正需要多项大规模的基建来建设城市的核心竞争力，于是他加入了这个行业，抓住了契机，事业后来逐步发展并壮大。我们家族最初进入这个行业做的就是预制混凝土、管道、水泥和花砖，见证了中国香港由工业建筑到房地产的繁荣发展。当中，我们重新审视了大企业的角色，并尝试多元化发展，酒店业是对房地产的补充，也提升了地区的价值，这一观点逐渐成为人们的共识。这促使我们在进行整合开发时考虑到溢出效应，并综合考虑各种因素，我们就是这样进入酒店业的。在2002年，澳门开放娱乐博彩业，我们看到了商机。概括来说，我们与其他中国香港的成功故事一样：紧贴市场并把握机会。从建筑业转向房地产业，从酒店业转向娱乐业。

采访者：在澳门逐步开放和银河娱乐集团蓬勃发展的过程中，是什么维持着您的热情、兴趣和动力?

受访者：我们相信我们有能力把娱乐业、博彩业和酒店业结合起来，发展成一个"超级产业"，当时在亚洲还没有谁完成过这样的事业。放眼世界，做到这一点的只有拉斯维加斯。当我在加州上学时，离拉斯维加斯不远，看着它从一个只有博彩业的小镇演变成一个集会展、零售、生活时尚、休闲、餐饮以及涵盖不同用餐体验的超级产业。见证这一演变过程后，我们相信在亚洲同样可以上演。我们相信这个可能性，并朝着这个方向努力。十分幸运，我们获批了博彩经营批给合同，我们也看到一个愿望——这仍然是一个愿望——即成为亚洲顶级娱乐公司之一。我们觉得，有了这个机会，而且也已对准了正确的市场去取得成功，这就是我们最初的动力来源。随着公司规模越来越大，而中国有 14 亿人口，澳门则是唯一博彩合法的地方，因此我们相信市场的未来潜力巨大。举个例子，在 2014 年，中国的中产市场规模就已达 4000 万人，在 20 年内可能会达到 6 亿，他们都是潜在客户。由此我们认为我们有能力成为举足轻重的企业。

采访者：您认为领导力的关键是什么？

受访者：我从没细想过自己的动力是来自某件事还是热情。当然，如果你没有热情的话，什么事情也做不了。你可能拥有世上的一切天赋、你可能是最聪明的人、你也可能有着远大理想，然而，如果你没有热情，我不认为你会有很大成就，因为成功是痛苦并快乐的一个过程。你不仅要激励自己，还要激励周边的人。当你身边有 22000 人（银娱有超过 22000 名员工），如果大家都会受你的愿景所影响，从而朝着同一个方向前进，这其实颇具挑战性，因为这需要巨大的热情，也需要很好的沟通方式。你得简明阐述自己的愿景，这样你的团队成员才能像你本人一样去理解和执行。正因为热情这个原因，我们才能在短时间内得到今天的成果。

采访者：我感觉您对餐饮业有着极大的关注和热情，在我们执教的酒店业院校（如香港理工大学），主厨富有创造力，餐饮从业者也充满热情。虽然您有着与之不同的工科背景，但显然怀有同样的热忱。

受访者：我想，无论是餐馆老板还是工程师，都需要热情才能有所成就。我愿意为我做的每一样工作付出 110% 的努力，没有这样的动力，是不可能成功的。如果你完成一项工作时只达到了目标的 80%，那其实好不过大多数人。大多数人可以达到 80%，我们需要的是愿意"付出额外努力"的人，这才是挑战所在。

采访者：您能举一些用来描述自己或者其他人描述您时可能使用的词吗？

受访者：为了让身边的人愿意跟随着你一起工作，正直和公平是至关重要的。你必须关注每个人以确保他们以应有的方式投入工作，同时不能表现出偏袒。公平对待每个人对于一位领导者来说十分重要。对我来说，只要员工表现好，就要给予奖励。同时，我会强调沟通，如果你不能确保持续沟通，那就无法实现你的目标。你必须耐心聆听别人的意见。对许多老板而言，沟通基本上是单向的。我所说的沟通，意思是你需要耐心和团队成员坐在一起，看着他们的眼睛，倾听他们所讲的话。

采访者： 在我们的领域内外，哪位领袖是您较为敬佩的？

受访者： 许多成功的商人和世界领袖都很励志。但要问谁对我的影响最大，那一定是我的父母。我的父亲是个非常严厉、非常传统的中国人。同时，在这样的中国家庭里，我母亲对我的一生有着很大的影响，她算得上是无名英雄。我猜每个年轻人被人指手画脚时都会有叛逆之心。如果纪律是以爱为出发点，人们其实是可以产生共鸣的。每个人都是独特的，但仍可以朝一个目标共同努力，这是我母亲教我的，如果我当时走上另一条叛逆之路，我应该不会有今天的成功。

采访者： 银娱的第三、第四期计划非常吸引人。您在珠海横琴岛和亚洲其他景点也有开发用地。澳门以外的发展和中国内地会如何结合？

受访者： 首先，我们需要富有创造力。如果你要获得可持续的成功，就必须建立自己的品牌形象和竞争优势。不得不说，来澳门的客人与其他地方的客人有很大的不同，我们必须以他们为核心，了解他们的需求是什么？他们的饮酒文化是否与美国人或者其他地方的人一样？他们的饮食习惯相同吗？他们对设施的需求一致吗？如果答案是否定的，那么你必须提供一个舒适、便捷的选择。我们在澳门取得成功的一部分原因是我们的设施适合用户，客人来到澳门银河会有宾至如归的感觉。

我还记得，大约15年前，许多人对我说这种方法走不通。不应该做这个，不应该放那个，房间必须得这么大，必须有很多酒吧，但我认为我们的客人不需要这些。在我开始接手银娱之前，我的任务是为家族开拓中国内地的业务，所以我在上海、广州和北京都生活过一段时间。我认为，要仔细了解客人所需，才能打造他们喜爱的服务和设施。我们的房型规格和西方同行不同，当顾问来的时候，他们就说我们的客人需要这个、需要那个，我们回答说："亚洲建筑偏小，所以没必要用同样规格的房间。"我的意思是，房间的内在可以小一些，但也许客人需要更多种类的设施，比如热水壶。我不知道你是否试过走进酒店房间时面前摆着茶壶，旁边还有泡面。我们是第一家在澳门这样做的酒店。我也是第一个提出娱乐场应该保持光亮的人，还记得过去的赌场总设在地下室，仿佛在告诉我不要进去，因为这样的环境不会让人感到快乐。而且一旦你进入后就很难走出来，因为那就像漆黑的迷宫一样。但是如果你走进银娱旗下的娱乐场所时，都是很明亮的，让人感觉舒适和积极，我希望大家都能来这里放松自我。因此，我们采用明亮的灯光和天窗，这样可以让自然光照进来。然而我仍然记得我被灌输过这样的思想：赌场里不应该有时间感，也不应该有时钟。一旦顾客进去就应该忘记时间，但我们没有这样做。现在，你可以看到新建的其他娱乐场也开始效仿我们了。

采访者： 随着公司的扩张，"傲视世界，情系亚洲"这一概念会继续适用吗？公司的精神是否需要调整，特别是在进军日本和其他地区以后。

受访者： 当我考虑为旗下项目树立服务宗旨时，"傲视世界，情系亚洲"应运而生。我们想表达的是，如果我们想做好一件事，就要做到国际水平。它应该有着丰富的内涵，允许你去领导市场。去过全世界不同地方后，我得到的印象是，亚洲的款客服务始终是最周到和贴心的。虽然这句话最初更多的是用于项目的服务层面，但后来逐渐被赋予更多的含义，并发展成了公司文化。这就是为什么"傲视世界，情系亚洲"不仅仅是一句浮于表面的座右铭，它更事关银娱的愿景——在所做的每一方面都做到世界级，这个理念已经不限于客户服务。

而亚洲的包罗万象思想亦融入了我们的硬件和设计。我希望能够突出我们立足于亚洲，特别是针对中国客群的定位。中国现在是世界第二大经济体，中产阶级正在快速增长，我们的国家让我们引以为傲，并拥有许多"财富"500强公司。我们想要做的是，可以向下一代说："这是我们留下来的成果。"大多数中国人想要的是摩登、现代和时尚的东西，同时还具备中国传统文化的内涵。因此，我认为"情系亚洲"的想法现在有了更多的意义。我们终于明白坚持本民族文化传统的优势所在。"情系亚洲"不仅涵盖了我们的服务和员工，还包含一套完整的观念模式：在规划、设计和解读中涉及更多的中国传统文化。我认为我们成功地做到了这一点，因为当你身处我们旗下的项目时，你会发现很多顶级、时尚和现代的中国或者亚洲元素。当你深入观察，你可以感受到更多中国元素，例如，澳门银河的一期和二期项目是以孔雀为设计概念——我们的许多设计都来源于孔雀，对我们来说，这是一件非常能体现亚洲文化的事情，因为对于亚洲人来说，孔雀象征着和平和财富。

采访者： 纵观粤港澳大湾区，香港是一个知名的城市。随着博彩业的开放，澳门的知名度也越来越高。现在，作为具有潜力的综合目的地，深圳正在快速发展。粤港澳大湾区有七八千万人。现代科技为城市之间的联系提供了便利，未来看起来很美好。几座城市通过相互连接彼此协作并产生足够的能量共同前进。

受访者： 我相信这会产生乘数效应。大概二三十年前，广州和东莞是中国香港的工业中心，但随后重心转移到了上海和长三角地区。在过去的 20 年里，上海的商贸蓬勃发展。然而，整个广东省正在复苏，重现活力。作为新兴经济的基础，技术正受到广泛应用。只要我们在未来 20 年做出正确的决策，就能够保持长远的竞争力。我还记得在被广东取代之前，北京一直是科技中心；现在，广东坐拥腾讯和华为等主流公司，香港为商业中心，深圳为科技中心，澳门为娱乐中心，当它们合为一体时会变得无比强大，而粤港澳是能够媲美旧金山湾区和东京湾区的。在"一国两制"制度体系下，我认为香港人有很多机会来做一些大事，我们应该认真教导我们的下一代和学生应如何善用这样的机会。我真希望我能年轻 40 岁！正如我记得 20 世纪 60、70、80 年代，中国香港有着很多机会，正是这些机会成就了我们如今的财富。试想一下，将来粤港澳大湾区的国内生产总值将再翻上几倍，我们应如何利用这一点？我们应该教育人们，让他们不害怕与内地人竞争。我们在这里实行"一国两制"。只要年青一代接受中国语言和文化，他们就能更好地理解和接纳中国香港、深圳和澳门之间的差异。在粤港澳大湾区各地，我看到了许多为年轻人准备的创业打拼的机会。

采访者： 也许我可以分享一下金融、科技和旅游业之间的联系。在杭州有许多大四学生就读于香港理工大学酒店和旅游管理学院，这是和浙江大学的合作项目，包括 100 名酒店和旅游管理专业的博士生和 130 名硕士生。飞猪旅行（阿里巴巴）的许多领导都在攻读硕士和博士学位。为什么？因为支付宝一向是一家科技和金融公司，他们希望找到能通过旅游业和酒店业将科技和金融巧妙结合的方法。

受访者： 人工智能（AI）对于我们的款客业务来说是很大的助力，尽管目前我们对其的应用只是表面，是很有限的了解，我们也正在深化对人工智能可以如何促进业务的理解。香港一直是金融中心，而金融、科技和旅游这三个要素的结合会产生巨大的效果。

采访者： 当今酒店业领导人面临的挑战与之前几代面临的挑战相同吗？相比之前的领导人，有哪些事情更应该被认真对待？

受访者： 也许年轻人面临的最大挑战是他们不像我们那么渴求机会。我们出生在 20 世纪五六十年代，那时香港并不发达，我们一心向上爬，满怀渴望，随时准备抓住一切工作机会。某种程度上，现在的年轻人没有同样的渴望去追求卓越。对我来说，这事关自律，这也是我强调热情的原因。

我父亲和家人以不同形式去积极支持和捐献不同的高等学府，还设立了吕志和奖，并宣布注资 13 亿港元成立银娱基金会，这笔款项的其中一个用途，是帮助年轻人在澳门及中国各地大展拳脚。我们对遇到的机会心怀感激。回到原来的问题，我认为我们为下一代设立了太多的保护，另一点是当年我们只有香港内部竞争，但改革开放 40 多年来，中国经济指数增长，我们正与 14 亿内地人竞争，我们的年轻人应该明白，现时有很多如饥似渴的内地年轻人正在努力赶超我们，所以我们需要迎接挑战。中国香港拥有很好的教育机构，也有很棒的商业体系。我认为只要我们的年轻人迎接挑战，多学习内地文化，学会如何在中国内地做生意，他们就会拥有很多机会。

采访者： 您的领导风格是什么？

受访者： 我简要地谈谈我的领导风格。我尊重所有的同事，主动给予他们支持，甚至为他们做得更多，这不仅仅是为了钱。虽然必须给团队成员发放工资，但被认可也是很重要的。团队成员应该要能感受到你的关心。这对我来说很重要。我们希望他们感到自豪。

谢谢你的提问，这让我有时间认真思考如何把事情做得更好。

PREFACE

Asia is well established as the world's fastest growing tourism region (PATA 2019). China has been the main driver of growth within the Asia region and continent, with tourism expanding on an unprecedented scale from, into and within the country. China's impact extends beyond visitor numbers and expenditures into tourism investments. As part of President Xi Jinping's Belt and Road Initiative, the influence of China is extending across the countries of the Silk Road Economic Belt and 21st Century Maritime Silk Road. In the face of such growing influence and the challenging thing about where to invest and to manage the rapid growth of tourism, it is timely to acquire a better understanding of the strategies being adopted by Chinese hospitality leaders both within and beyond the country. It is self-evident that there will be greater expectations of those who are leading the various initiatives in the face of rapid growth (Smith & Sigauw, 2011).

The origins of the present volume were a shared interest on the part of the three co- authors in cultivating and expanding Chinese hospitality leadership capacities. The three authors are associated with the School of Hotel and Tourism Management (SHTM) at The Hong Kong Polytechnic University and their views have been shaped through teaching successive cohorts of undergraduate and postgraduate hospitality students, as well as engaging in training of hospitality executives. They have authored previous hospitality and tourism books that involved interviewing industry leaders with a view to acquiring insights. It is the authors' view that SHTM is ideally placed as a starting point for the present investigation. Firstly, the research that underpins the volume was funded by the School. Secondly, the School is led by Professor Kaye Chon who is Dean and he has pioneered the concept of an "Asian wave" of tourism and hospitality and the "Asian paradigm" concept (Chon 2014, 2018). The inclusion of Dean Chon as one of the interviewees and key informants for the book embeds the hospitality education perspective in this exploration of leadership concepts and the modelling of emerging Asian "best practices" in leadership.

This purposeful China focus of the book should enable readers to learn about leadership theories and practice from a variety of prominent Chinese "voices".

To reinforce the centrality of the Chinese perspective, the authors have opted to present this volume bilingually. This approach was partly informed by the authors' experience of bilingual teaching to students in China. Through a partnership with Zhejiang University in Hangzhou that dates back over 15 years, PolyU faculty deliver an MSc degree in Hotel and Tourism Management and a Doctor of Hotel and Tourism Management (D.HTM) to students who are typically seasoned industry executives. Since the students' average length of industry experience is nine years, the learning style resembles executive education. The various subject professors conduct all classes in Chinese, though the written materials for class are presented in both Chinese and English. The many years of delivering advanced-level postgraduate hospitality education to successful graduation has produced an extensive alumni network across China. Some of these alumni were interviewed for the purposes of the present volume. These sessions built upon the earlier paper by one of the current authors that advanced the concept of progressing professionalism within hospitality (Cheng and Wong, 2015).

Noting the rapid growth of tourism, the authors attest the need to deeply understand prevailing hospitality leadership strategies. If the momentum is to be maintained in a sustainable manner, it will be important to acquire insights from those who have already taken on leadership responsibilities. This book addresses such issues by providing readers with insights into the innovative approaches that have been adopted by hospitality and tourism leaders across greater China.

The book includes a series of interviews with industry leaders that are presented bilingually. Each of the various book chapters originated as tape-recorded interviews with industry leaders. Authors/interviewers adopted a semi-structured format based on a series of common questions, though the capacity to adapt the line of inquiry in response to changing circumstances and to the needs and preferences of each interviewee. The interviews were conducted in either English or in Chinese at the offices of the various respondents at the preference of the respondent. Interviewing was undertaken face-to-face in all cases except for one case where teleconferencing was used. Respondents are "C-level" within their respective organizations, typically at the level of Chief Executive Officer (CEO), Chair, Founder or Vice President.

The authors investigate the impact of organizational settings on the exercise of leadership, though noting the strong connection between individual leadership characteristics and organizational factors. The authors also wished to bring out different perspectives of both female and male leaders. Of the nine interviewees, four are women and five are men. For future leadership, this was a viewed as an important issue since most (70%) of current cohort of hospitality students are women and it is essential to understand the challenges and opportunities ahead for them.

As part of the scientific research process, the authors sought to develop a line of questioning by firstly scanning the relevant hospitality leadership literature and secondly seeking insights about leadership from the cohort of postgraduate hospitality students in China, most of whom have already acquired substantial experience in leading hotel companies. For purposes of research piloting, the authors conducted a series of focus group interviews in Hangzhou and in Shenzhen. The reports of these interviews have already been documented in the academic literature (Cheung, King and Wong, 2018). As an outlet for this component of the research, the authors purposefully targeted the *Journal of China Tourism Research* (JCTR). JCTR is unique amongst the 200+ hospitality and tourism academic journals since the abstracts of all papers are presented in both Chinese and English. The paper highlighted the most admired senior hospitality leaders in China from the perspective of middle managers and identified leadership traits and characteristics that are viewed as being well suited to Chinese circumstances.

The participants of the focus group were distinguished by the time and resources that have been committed to a potential future in the industry through study. The perspectives of these aspirant leaders about the future are particularly interesting given the increasing emphasis on experiential learning as a preparation for hospitality leadership (Jian and Cheung 2013). Previous literature has suggested that their preferred managerial activities would provide potentially valuable insights (Waryszak and King, 2001). Since the SHTM China alumni are a growing and influential group, it was also felt that their perspectives on leadership could produce valuable insights for the future of hospitality management education.

Based on the findings of the various focus group, the following questions were formulated to draw out the best insights from the various respondents as major investigative themes:

How have the various respondents achieved a position of leadership and coped wiht competition?

What challenges respondents believe will confront the upcoming generation of Chinese tourism leaders?

What are the particularities of the leadership that characterize the hospitality and tourism sub-sector which the respondent represents?

How have different organizational types shaped leadership, notably in the case of state-owned enterprises, family businesses and transnational corporations?

How have respondent organizations accommodated the preferences of customers and business partners from different ethnic, cultural and geographic backgrounds?

Are there challenges of succession planning and generational change as the current crop of leaders progressively gives way to a new generation (the Millennials)?

By providing readers with rich insights from admired senior leaders about their personal and organizational experiences, it is hoped that this book will be of interest to industry practitioners, to students and to scholars.

Brian King

In January 2020

Challenges for Hospitality Leadership in State-owned Enterprises

Interviewee: Mr. Chen Xueming
Title: CEO of Nanjing Jinling Hotel Corporation
Interviewer: Dr. Alan Wong

Interviewer: Could you talk about your motivation to join the hospitality industry, Mr. Chen?

Interviewee: My background was very interesting. I started my career on 15th May 1978 at the Jinjiang Hotel which in Shanghai and I worked for five and a half years as a Western cook. Which I then applied to the Shanghai Institute of Tourism, the oldest tourism school in China. Following my graduation, the Jinjiang Hotel appointed me as committee secretary of the youth corps. I also had the opportunity of a government scholarship to study in Germany. I spent approximately two years there, learning about hospitality management. After my graduation in 1989, I returned to a marketing role with Jinjiang. After starting as sales manager I went through various promotions to reach the role of CEO. I served in the roles of Deputy General Manager, General Manager, and Legal Representative of the Shanghai Jinjiang Hotel, of Beijing International Hotel, Shanghai Longbai Hotel, Shanghai International Convention Center Hotel, and the Shanghai Everbright Convention and Exhibition Center. I also served as the director with two real estate companies. I joined Nanjing Jinling hotel management company in March 2011, and currently serve as CEO. I have now been working in this industry for nearly 39 years.

Interviewer: Why did you first enter the hospitality industry, and how?

Interviewee: For my first job, the government assigned me to the hotel industry. Once I started my internship at the Four Seasons in Hamburg, Germany I decided to become a professional hotel manager. The Four Seasons Hamburg is a top in the world, arguably the best in Europe. I was greatly inspired by the internship experience and realized that Chinese could manage hotels just as well as Germans. This belief has always encouraged me. I have had the opportunity to manage a variety of types of hotel — large international properties, specialty boutique hotels, conference hotels, exhibition hotels and VIP floors. I chose to join and operate a hotel chain - Jinling - as a way of capitalizing on the wealth of experience that I had acquired managing individual hotels.

I attach greatest pride to having directed two state banquets in two cities. In 1999, in the case of the first state banquet General Secretary Jiang Zemin participated, along with representatives from Fortune 500 companies. In Shanghai. In 2014, the Youth Olympic Games were staged in Nanjing. President Xi Jinping and Premier Li Keqiang participated in the ceremony. The preparation for the banquet was very tough and I was under great pressure. It was a terrific experience and a rare opportunity for me.

Interviewer: What keeps you motivated?

Interviewee: There is a kind of Chinese national sentiment which inspired me and encouraged me to keep moving forward. The Chinese hospitality industry was still very backward and undeveloped during the early 1980s. I learned a lot when I studied in Germany. Two things particularly impressed me during my time at the Four Seasons in Hamburg. The first was that the hotel never offered discounts, because they thought their service was perfect and faultless. There was no reason that they should give a discount for their perfect service. That meant the service quality hotel price should set the price. I would like to mention another case. One day, a walk-in guest approached the front desk and asked, "Do you have available rooms?" Although the hotel had rooms available, my manager said to the guest, "We are full". I was very surprised and later asked him the reason why he had said that. My manager didn't answer my question but instead asked me, "Do you know who he is?" Suddenly, I understood, because as one of the world's best hotels, we needed to know each of our customers through precise target marketing.

We won't serve anyone other than our guests. I have become successful by using the concepts behind these two cases to manage the Jinjiang Longbai Hotel and the Jinjiang VIP Tower. And I have made a success in doing this than foreign managers.

I undertook a second internship in the Best Western Hotel in Germany, which was worth comparing it with the Four Seasons Hotel. The Four Seasons has 145 rooms with 400 employees and the Best Western hotel has 105 rooms and only 18 employees. Despite this, it provides a very good service and controls its costs effectively. This indicates that the number of employees is not the key to success in the hotel business. Built by Jinling Hotel Group, I would like to use such a strategy to a hotel sub-brand in the near future. My dream has been to follow the operational models for the Four Seasons and Best Western to roll out our own hotel operations model - Jinjiang Century City has followed the Four Seasons Model. The other hotel will follow the Best Western approach. We will make another dream come true in due course. In the first-tier cities we have probably not yet caught up with the foreign hotel brands. However, we will soon surpass the international brand hotels in the second and third-tier cities.

Interviewer: Could you summarize the key characteristics of hospitality leadership?

Interviewee: Leadership is getting others to help you to do what you want to do. In my understanding, the largest cost of management is trust. The goal of customer relationship management in hospitality is to create trust, including trust between the leader and the staff. Your leadership and management will succeed when you earn their trust. Such trust is not obtained through authority, but by your good conduct. Since hospitality is not a high-tech industry, our job involves dealing with the relationships between people. All hotel work concerns dealing with relationships, and good relationships mean productivity. We can only handle the various relationships when the staff trust us. It involves a variety of elements, and your leadership depends on whether you can acquire and retain the trust of your team members.

Interviewer: Is hospitality leadership different from leadership in other industries and if so what are the differences? How do you build trust within your team?

Interviewee: The difference lies in the strong capabilities that we have in the hospitality industry about cultivating and managing relationships. We know how to size up situations and to nurture relationships with others. A hotel is a place where everyone feels happy and the industry needs generalists, not professionals. The subordinates within my team will not be angry if I scold them. That is because of "goodwill." We have worked together for a long time, and they know my three principles: 1. I will not make hard on employees (this unavoidably creates difficulties and makes a person uncomfortable); 2. I will not deduct their wages and benefits; and 3. I will provide them with good opportunities.

Interviewer: Are you faced with some special challenges as a leader in this field?

Interviewee: Firstly, I need to handle interpersonal relationships and to be able to get along with people.

Secondly, I need to truly understand the hotel industry and the nature of the enterprise, not just possess professional knowledge. Though each individual hotel has much in common with others, the characteristics are not identical. I need to find the distinct personality of hotels where I can see through the phenomenon to the essence. The depth of awareness of the enterprise will determine whether management of the business enterprise is successful.

Interviewer: You joined Jinling in 2011. How would you describe the differences between Jinling and Jinjiang?

Interviewee: Since the start of China's economic reforms and opening up, the focus of the hospitality industry has been on opening and developing hotels. Many foreign hotels have come in, but in China a hotel management company is not successful, and whether we are speaking of Jinjiang or Jinling, in fact, they are not successful. The reason why they are unsuccessful is that we confuse the concepts of a group and a chain. We need to examine the nature of the phenomenon. Jinjiang belongs to a group with the capital based of the organization serving as a link to the formation of a large-scale hotel group. The business finances belong to an internal financial statement and this should not be regarded as a chain. In a chain the report for each hotel does not come from the inside.

We provide a business model and receive a management fee. In other words, I think that the Chinese do not understand the problem with this hotel. The difference between a single hotel and a chain hotel may be explored by looking at a glass of water. In the case of a single hotel, whether 60% or 70% is better in the cup. For a chain hotel determining the same standard of water is the key.

The first of Peter Drucker's three rules is that you should know your business. In the end I have come to know what kind of business it is. Only with a deep understanding of its personality and requirements can you reach farther. Trust is basic. Professionalism forms a foundation which can slowly be accumulated and built upon. Then there will be a job. Many general managers will not oversee the work. In fact, management is about issuing tasks—the task of how to achieve the leadership and management capacity.

My point of view is that Han Xin a guiding philosophy of "the more the better" when recruiting his soldiers. Do not dictate the kind of person deliberately, since talent cannot be met. In playing only a good card, a person will confine him/herself. You can play a hand, irrespective of the set of cards in your hand,. Everyone has choices (plasticity). It is important to employ people and to teach them to avoid selling people short. As a leader, everyone has plasticity, and success is depends on whether the leader understands people and can deploy them well. When a work assignment depends on personal ability, I do not agree with the use of rewards and punishments, because that approach divides things into the good and the bad. It is subjective, rather than not objective. It easily creates controversy and arguments over who is or is not important. That produces chaotic business management.

Interviewer: Who is your most admired leader in hospitality and tourism?

Interviewee: My most admirable leader is Si Haiyan. He was initially a police officer, and was then sent by the Public Security Bureau to work at the hotel as the vice president. He also became hotel the general manager of Beijing Kunlun. He is a former president of the travel hotel association and has now retired. He proceeded step by step from being a layman to an expert and then to a wizard and master. He wrote a novel, which became a TV series. However, the thing about him most worth learning is that he was the operator of the hotel, and in terms of human management he has very unique and profound insights. His management is about love; his management style is strict also affectionate. I admire him greatly.

Interviewer: What is the difference between State-owned enterprises and private entenprises?

Interviewee: They are totally different. The leadership of state-owned enterprises is reflected in the rules of the game: The state leader wants to work in accordance with the superior, and they do not force innovation and efficiency, nor do they force the work to be vigorous and resolute. The state leader's greatest requirement is to avoid making mistakes. You can perform nine things right, as long as there is no one thing wrong. Therefore, the leadership of state-owned enterprises must have the ability to remain in accord with the rules governing what to do. By contrast, private enterprises prioritize effectiveness and efficiency first, the priority of state-owned enterprises is compliance. If I am in a state owned company, even in a market-oriented division, I would need to be an effective coordinator in order to make tradeoffs between efficiency and making errors. This would be my biggest challenge. I cannot give exclusive attention to the pursuit of efficiency. If there is something in the report about a connection, it will never be implemented as long as "a ring is stuck". It is difficult to unify the ideas since everyone has a different starting point and perspective about what should be considered. National policy governs state-owned enterprises and guides the outline of their work. Private enterprises have greater flexibility about how to do things, albeit in accordance with their internal policies and according to the law of the country.

Interviewer: How do you keep your team motivated for market leadership?

Interviewee: It is my view that we should be outstanding in something-one area. The overall market image of Jinling was confusing because they operated a no-frills ("shortcut") chain brand, "Jin a village," through a franchise mode. Since the operating capacity of the company is limited, I have adopted a focused strategy, using "Jinling," of a single and unified brand. I describe the business operation as an "entrusted management model," and it is no longer a franchise. I am pursuing a single investment approach, consistent with the view that one should " … not invest only in asset-light chain management." This clarifies the market image of Jinling, leading others to associate us with high-end hotels when they think of us. This status is now recognized by the industry, and other local chain hotels aspire to be like Jinling.

Interviewer: How should leadership be passed on to upcoming generations?

Interviewee: First of all, leaders should lead by example, and embody a love of the industry and transmit this to others. Besides, you need to pass on your hotel knowledge through effective delivery. Every year I do several keynote speeches to our group, sharing my knowledge of the hotel to those who are next in line. It's also the case that your smile and language can be infectious to others when you are positive. We hope that our Jinling team spreads goodwill, by acting like a big family. Finally, leadership is the ability to inspire others to deal with problems. Professional knowledge can be accumulated through learning, but leadership is more about practing and exposuring to reality — leadership is not learned in a classroom.

Interviewer: How would you describe corporate culture in your group?

Interviewee: We have created a special Jinling corporate culture. I always acknowledge the importance of education. However, I believe that leadership cannot be learnt through lectures. Why accept the same education, with the same class consisting of a few people? More time should be spent on practice, outside the classroom. I try to give students inspiration. Inspiration is more important than education per se.

Interviewer: How do you think about the challenges for the industry?

Interviewee: I think that cultural conflict is the main challenge. For example, foreigners behave directly, whereas Chinese do not. The Chinese people pay attention to face, and foreigners are different. Because of such cultural differences and potential conflicts, sending mainlanders to Hong Kong to learn about hotel management is not enough. Foreigners can manage hotels in first-tier cities, with their international stand-ards. However, in second- and third-tier cities, the former foreign managers have gone and all of the hotels are using a localization strategy because of problems with cultural conflicts. In response to this challenge I have been advocating localization. The manage hotels in the region because people who are of the region can the best. If there is no basis for cultural understanding, the hotel is not a good cross-regional hotel.

Interviewer: What are the biggest challenges that will confront future leaders?

Interviewee: The biggest challenge is the need to have a very strong capacity to integrate. This is such a challenge because we are a chain that is also a professional manager. Everyone comes from different environments and backgrounds, leading to disparate values. As a business leader you must integrate them all together, so that everyone who is seeking to work in Datong stays consistent. If you cannot integrate effectively, then you will need to make changes to the business. Fusion is acceptable, though you should not give up your individuality.

Interviewer: Do you think that leadership innovation is important?

Interviewee: I think that innovation is not the most important thing nor the leading aspect. General enterprises have three categories: basic staff, experts, and leaders. In the industry that specializes in innovation, this function is undertaken by experts. Steve Jobs was not an innovator. Rather than relying on his own innovation, his success derived from selecting from amongst 1,000 projects, namely the three that we all recognize. Leadership is more the face of management, and innovation should be for the experts. Leadership should encompass integration and management. For the latter the most important thing is managing good people.

Interviewer: What challenges do globalization bring to the Chinese hotel industry?

Interviewee: The biggest challenge is that awareness of local high-end hotel chains remains backward and insufficient in China. None is discussing the value of the local high-end hotel chains, or impressing foreigners, even though economic growth has led to the development of a more mature hotel sector. China is that most deficient in shining its own national light on the assets of the high-end luxury hotel chains and this is a huge challenge for those of us who are involved. Professional managers and capital owners come from different perspectives. Professional managers are not the right people to invest, and the investment business people should give more consideration to the value-added capacity of their own assets. Though they are learning, there is insufficient understanding of the chains and groups. Their focus is more on the overall shape, but not the nature of the chain.

Interviewer: How are issues of gender, the new generation, and the aging population impacting on your business?

Interviewee: Hotels are a sunrise industry, and the hotel industry will not die as long as there is a flow of business. The market adjusts to supply and demand, and the hotels are still operating, despite our talk about the lack of people. The pay is constantly improving, and in the end, owners will always pay someone who is willing to come. So pay is not a factor. In terms of gender I would describe hotels are more of a "female industry". Investment issues may be more suitable for men, but with regard to the management and the treatment of people, women will be more appropriate than men and also will be more meticulous. On the issue of leadership, there are always people willing to be the leader. I also believe that without happy employees, there can be no satisfied customers.

Interviewer: What are the characteristics of state-owned enterprises?

Interviewee: Leadership is weaker in state-owned enterprises, and is determined by your position and level. When you take up a particular position, you do not need to demonstrate leadership, but administrative capacity. With my title in a state-owned enterprise, I will pay more attention to the rules. There is a strong sense of leadership in China, with the belief that the outstanding usually besr the brunt of acttack. For Jinling's state-owned enterprises, the biggest contradiction is the nature of the market and the coordination of the enterprise. In my work, sometimes I cannot speak about full compliance, I cannot talk about efficiency and efficiency. For example, we want to set up subordinate companies, but the state provides state-owned holding companies that cannot set up four companies. How can I coordinate that? I could sign someone to do the project, and then I would follow our regular form of cooperation, but without the essence of the contents of the company or the mode of operation. Although relatively reluctantly, things can be made to happen.

Interviewer: Should leaders have the capacity to learn?

Interviewee: Of course. The first priority is to learn, to follow the changes in the world, to study the strains and stresses, to read articles and understand how the changes are generated, and after learning to think about what you learned.

Secrets of Cross-disciplinary Leadership

Interviewee: Ms. Jin Du
Title: Founder of Home Away from Home Resort
Interviewer: Dr. Alan Wong

Interviewer: How did you change careers from media to hospitality industry?

Interviewee: My study major at University was in journalism, from bachelor to master. I won the Tao Fen news award when I was a postgraduate student, the highest award in the journalism industry. Prior to my graduation I was assigned to the South Daily News Group and I worked there for 15 years. The enterprise identified me as the key person for training and development.

Interviewer: How did you get into this industry?

Interviewee: The first reason was my personal interest. I feel that it is important to love something from your heart and I know that this is what I like. You can perform your best when you enjoy what you are doing. I only recruit staff who enjoy traveling and communicating. If they don't have these qualities then I won't hire them.

The second reason prompting me to go into hospitality industry was timing. I had been working in the media industry for 15 years. I had achieved quite a senior position and felt that this was enough in the particular field. You might also say that I had hit the "glass ceiling". I also had a feeling that this industry was and is going downhill.

The third reason was a wish to try out something new. I wanted to do something different in my spare time. This prompted me to invest in a homestay hotel in Erhai, Yunnan along with five of my friends. The project progressed smoothly, from the site selection, to signing a contract, doing the decorations and then the opening. The occupancy rate is about 95% which shows the popularity. The project won this year's China Design: Small Hotel Award. I think that this brings me greater happiness than making more money.

The homestay concept was also something that drew me to hospitality. My primary purpose was not to make money. I think of education as allowing the brain to explore, and traveling as allowing one's cognition to explore. These reasons prompted me to invest in education and in travel. I have found there is no leading-level homestay brand. This means that there are no rules that must be followed to keep up. I was curious whether the successful business model of my initial homestay could be repeated elsewhere. I had already identified this as my business direction at an early stage. The idea of investing time to understand theories applicable to hospitality also gave me some impetus. I sought advice from Dr Alan Wong about study when I was serving as General Manager of Advertising at Southern Newspapers. I asked Dr Wong whether I should acquire a degree from a hospitality school and he recommended that I should do so. I undertook some initial preparations to progress my business idea and model. First I made a "demo" and this proved to be successful. Secondly, I studied at SHTM, PolyU to learn about the thinking of hoteliers and the related theories. Thirdly, because I was a seasoned and experienced journalist, I could quickly become acquainted with an industry by communicating with industry professionals. This was my advantage. My friends confirmed my own thinking by advising me to enter the tourism and hospitality industry because I have a way of thinking that is different from others and am good at problem solving. I proposed a "five-one model" for my homestay. The elements consist of: one hometown, one (terrific) homestay, one trip, one product and one community. I have also obtained investments from Ying Luo and the Platinum Group.

Interviewer: What are the characteristics of leaders in the hospitality and other service sectors? Are these different from what prevails in other industries?

Interviewee: They are almost the same since the key is always about motivating employees and teams. However the best approach varies in different industries. For instance, in the Southern News Group, the staff are all high-level intellectuals with a strong capacity to manage themselves. This leads to a more relaxed style of management style which is not strict. However, the hospitality industry is labor-intensive and the employees are at relatively lower educational levels. This is a particular challenge for me, because I think the should magage themselves I hope that staff will work efficiently and live earnestly - I don't like ineffective overtime. The product that we are offering and running is highly experiential. We can only touch the feelings of our customers when we are enjoying our own lives.

The aspect of human resources was a particular challenge when I was starting my business. I found it hard to recruit qualified staff. Whilst many founders of startups seek help from their relatives and friends, I have none in Guangzhou. This prompted me to use a new approach to solve the problem. Everyone in our company adores me and supports the corporate culture. First, I have appeal, and I recruit employees who have a proven ability to motivate and drive themselves. They must have a specific dream, such as wanting to open a hotel and to be interested in learning from me. I hope that my homestay brand can ultimately become a platform which will allow the sharing of financial resources, recruitment methods, and management styles. This platform should also help people like me to achieve their dreams. My rule is to prioritize the user experience, though I share the profits with my staff. Also, I cannot accept complaints. Because of our priority on customer feelings, we engage in strict checking of our recommended products. Thus, my colleagues share my values. We place high demands on our hotel managers. My company embraces innovation. I draw up a staff growth plan at the start of each year. For example, if you want to earn a higher salary this year, you will need to put in more effort. I also allow staff to take leave during the off-season. This provides better social opportunities and more adaptability for those who love to travel.

Interviewer: Do private and state-owned enterprises have different leadership requirements? Is leadership more influenced by personal or by organizational factors?

Interviewee: At the beginning, I joined Southern News Group because of the personal charisma of the Chief Editor. He said that we were not there to write articles, but to rewrite the social process. Young people really have a dream – without this it is hard to find value in your work and easy to become bored. I regard the power of the dream as important, and believe that team cohesion is strongest when team members experience the pain and challenges together.

Later, because of organizational expansion, the process of management becomes longer and there is more "KP" (kitchen police), which I dislike. I hope that my company will never have more than 50 employees. I believe that high sales can be created by a small-scale company. The key is how to innovate the organizational model. Additionally I believe that the most important thing for success in business and management is your insight into human nature.

Interviewer: Who is your most admired leader?

Interviewee: My most admired leader is Zheng Nanyan who founded the Platinum Group. He is from the IT industry and operates his business with people who do not have hotel backgrounds. I agree with him that healthier organizations are in an unstable state, because this leads to innovation. I admire him, because I think that true entrepreneurs are very lonely. The founder and leader must be able to compress their energies and to drive themselves. Not everyone is able to endure the stress that is involved. Thus, I need to communicate with entrepreneurs to ease up.

I think that Zheng can see the essence through the phenomenon. He can seize your thoughts in a brief time. He once invited me to join the Platinum Group, but I refused. When he wanted to invest in my company, I asked him three questions.

The first question:"Why should I accept your investment?" He said: "The Platinum Group would like to hold more of your shares, which is a standard business behavior, but I can also understand you from your perspective as the founder. To solve this problem, the Platinum Group will only acquire 10% of your shares. Also, we do not need to be a leader, and you do not have to be the Platinum Group Brand." These words dispelled my initial concerns.

The second question I asked him was, "What are the benefits to me of you investing in my company?" He said, "Whilst there is no benefit when you are doing well, we can help you when you experience difficulties." I think that he speaks frankly and to the point.

The third question I asked him was, "What are the requirements for me?" To that, he said, "There is no requirement, that is, you only need to interact with our executives every 2-3 months. Our executives understand that there are a lot of people with different ideas. I chose you because your way of thinking is different from ours. There may be a lot of blind spots that we cannot see, and maybe you see them." He made decisions very quickly.

I am a scholar-oriented entrepreneur. This is my greatest advantage, also a disadvantage. I would like to ask someone else's advice, study a course and/or write a business proposal before making decisions. Zheng Nanyan once told me that the entire business was not written down, nor was the business proposal. He said that you did so because of a lack of courage to start the business, and because of fear of failure. Business is an accumulation of countless defeats and is not deduced from what is written.

Another "angel investor" (an affluent individual who provides capital for a business start-up, usually in exchange for convertible debt or ownership equity) said that my biggest advantage is that I can rapidly grasp the general picture of an industry. However, this may lead me to think too much, leading to a lack of mobility.

Self-awareness is very important for the exercise of effective leadership. We need to know our strengths and weaknesses. Our company recruits by using the Belbin Role Test (a behavioural test which was devised to measure preference for nine Team Roles. We believe that there are no perfect people, but that there is a perfect team. A team needs variety: some who are cautious, some who are creative, and so on. We try to find a person's strengths and weaknesses, and then determine the appropriate position for that person. For example, for a person who loves to identify problems, you get them to do process monitoring. If a person has a lot of ideas, you let him do marketing, but not finance. To give less pressure, 70% of the tasks that I assign to them are what they are good at. The other 30% of their tasks are things with which they are unfamiliar.

Interviewer: So part of your success is to use the strengths of team members and to avoid applying too much pressure?

Interviewee: When tasks are too difficult team members fall quickly into self-denial. Younger people are seeking a sense of accomplishment and this is more important to them than money. They may be unhappy if you tell them how to do something. They will be more excited to find out what they have done on their own. If you let them try so that they succeed through their own efforts, they will be very happy. The team attraction is not from money and the boss. The most important thing is that members become increasingly confident through their work.

Interviewer: What do you feel about Guanxi(relationship)?

Interviewee: Today's business environment is different from before. We have no Guanxi at all in our organization. When I stand on stage to present my idea, people are very willing to cooperate with me. I need to use my appeal. For example, I shared my experience with the executive team at Country Garden. I told them about my suffering, about my challenges, and about my values and ideas. They feel that my ideas are dramatically different from those of traditional hotels. I was invited to do the sharing by my classmate, Ji Yongjun. He felt that I had important things to share with the executive team. It is a mutual sharing because I also like their pragmatic approach and business culture. The company is highly efficient and has strong execution.

Interviewer: How is the corporate culture in Home Away from Home Resort

Interviewee: We have a set of corporate values. The user experience is the first and most important element. It involves determining the basics by undertaking research. The second is to be concerned with small things - big things are composed of hundreds of small things. The third is to know how to share with others. I never fear when my subordinates negotiate salary and compensation with me. For example, when I was managing hundreds of salespeople at Southern Newspapers, the sales team would come to my office at the beginning of each year to set their expected salaries. I give each of my current staff 20 undeveloped customers from my database and ask them to tell me their research results after a month - who could be potential guests. I can then help them analyze how to get that customer - a "win-win" situation for both parties. I feel that empathy is particularly important. You not only need to think from the staff perspective, but also about the development of the enterprise. You must also consider the consumer perspective. I don't think that an enterprise can be successful if it only cares about the benefits for shareholders.

Interviewer: How can your generation leave a positive legacy for the next batch of leaders?

Interviewee: We have not yet encountered this problem. It is a problem for State-owned enterprises (SOEs) such as the Southern newspaper group. Previous leaders achieved success through their corporate values. However, the current leaders do not recognize such values and this is confusing for team members. The biggest problem for SOEs is that the leader does not select the successor. They are appointed by the organization. They will stay in the position for only 3-5 years, and give little consideration to the corporate values and to formulating a succession plan. The corporate culture often follows the leader's personal culture. If the leader is an introvert, he will tend to focus on efficient implementation. If the corporate leader is innovative, he will encourage innovation and adventure. There is a great difference across mainland state-owned enterprises. It is a kind of "leader's culture". In private enterprises such as Country Garden, it is a family culture.

Interviewer: Do you have succession planning in your organization?

Interviewee: Yes we do. It's relatively easy for us because we don't have many employees. We work together and the most important element is moral quality. We have a simple culture — don't make things bad in our organization. I view myself as a principled person — if you have accepted my assigned task, you have a responsibility to do it. If you don't do it, you will be punished. I think that commitment is important. If you keep your commitments, you do not have an unintended effect on others.

Interviewer: What current challenges confront those leading hospitality organizations in the contexts of mainland China, Hong Kong and Macao?

Interviewee: Though some of my younger employees have hotel experience, they have not worked in the five-star hotels because they can't learn from the work. The biggest challenge of the hospitality industry is that those born in the 1990s are totally different and dislike boring work. The biggest challenge is satisfying their passion and giving them a sense of accomplishment. Those born in the 1960s and 1970s have a sense of responsibility, whereas those from the 1990s do not. Most of them do not want to buy a house. Instead, they think about traveling round the world. They focus on communicating with customers. They like working in B&Bs because they like being a host and can be in charge of the business. Our managers are 20+ years old, and we created a girls' travel group which won a Universal Women's Innovation Award.

Interviewer: How did you get the idea for Girlfriends' travel?

Interviewee: We always think from the user perspective. Chinese women are paying increasing attention to personal growth and development. I travel every year with my friend and we share our experiences through this journey. I think that contemporary travel is highly complex and that we can learn while traveling. For that reason, we ask guests to sign up to our travel plan. The performance of our managers has been very outstanding in this activity. Even our guests want to stay on to be a manager!

Of all of the everyday consumer goods, 70% are made for women on the basis that women are the key decision-makers. They are the party with the purchasing behaviors. I understand female consumers because I am one of them. The Home Away from Home Resort doesn't have high sales volume, but has strong brand awareness in this industry. For me, the hotel industry is just a platform, and I get to meet more interesting people through this. I am also an integrator of resources - I coordinate a variety of resources and I do that best in the media industry.

The reason I can get along with younger people is that I give them greater autonomy. For example, I give them full authorization to design the trips, and only take responsible for the comments. I allow them to make mistakes on the understanding that you can make minor mistakes, though not big ones. You need to find ways to make up for a mistake, and should not make the same mistake repeatedly. A company cannot progress if you do not allow other people to make mistakes.

Young people also want to showcase themselves, as well as to enjoy a sense of accomplishment. They have a lots of opportunities in my company. They only need to follow 60%~70% of the SOPs, and must create the rest. They will need to convince me if they want a higher salary. If they cannot convince me, I will put them on a 10-day trial. I believe that inspiring people's dreams and knowing their demands is important— as important as it is to sell the consumer goods.

Interviewer: What about family relationships? How can you balance family with works?

Interviewee: My husband and I work in cooperation with an appropriate division of labor. He takes care of the family and of our son. However, he sometimes complains, because he feels that my work intensity is beyond his imagination.

I have my own perspective. Managing the family is the same as managing a company. My family members have strong execution and are responsible for implementation. I only tell them how to do things and help to set our goals. I made a chart for my son and assigned him different tasks. And I made a deal with him that would let him achieve the goals. He is only 6 years old and loves pizza. I will buy him a pizza if he can meet my requirements. For instance, he needs to do 7 tasks in 1 day and 49 tasks in a week. If he completes all the tasks, he gets 49 points. If he misses one task he loses 2 points. He can eat pizza if he gets 20 points or more. In his daily tasks, five are his strengths and two are not. He is now more self-disciplined than me. Sometimes I ask the family to join me on my business trips. I think that education involves words and deeds. My son will study hard when he sees that his mom is working hard. His self-management ability is very strong.

Interviewer: How do government policies affect your way of leading your organization?

Interviewee: I believe that governmental policies do influence leadership and affect the final income that flows to the organization. Also because policies change, this will tend to impact on the leadership.

Interviewer: What do you think are some of the key characteristics of successful leaders?

Interviewee: Being broadminded is the key. A leader's broadmindedness and tolerance will determine his popularity. We all have different personalities; you can't manage people in one way only. Everyone has strengths and weaknesses. A broadminded leader can put people in the place that is right for them. Though a leader may be wise, he can't be effective if he doesn't have a broad mind. For example, when my behavior offended Zheng Nanyan, he was not angry. This was because of his broadmindedness.

Interviewer: Will future leaders need to have a multidisciplinary (trans-boundary) capability?

Interviewee: I don't think so. A fundamental capacity of leaders is the capacity to see through appearances and to perceive the essence. That is, you need the core capability of insight into human nature. A multidisciplinary ability is only about knowledge. However, knowledge and skills are only a small barrier, and there are many industry experts with knowledge and skills. A capacity to observe is important - some people cannot see beyond the border, because they only have knowledge of a single industry and cannot get to the nature or root of the problem. For example, I asked the staff why Country Garden wants to cooperate with us. Our competitiveness is based on product differentiation, not because our products are cheap (low-cost). This provides a basis for judging the matter. When people are working in procurement, their first priority is cost. Knowing this will prompt me to ask them why Country Garden wish to cooperate with us. It should be because of the great added value that is provided by our ideas and concepts and by the packaging of our products. Why would you want to reduce our core competitiveness? That is the logic of seeing through the appearance and to perceiving the essence.

Building a Local Luxury Resort Brand through Core Chinese Values and Concepts

Interviewee: Mr. Wei Li
Title: Founder of WEI brand
Interviewer: Dr. Alan Wong

Interviewer: Why did you choose this industry?

Interviewee: Actually, it was during the year when I was looking for my first job that the hospitality industry became an option. At that time, there was only one foreign company - Holiday Inn – that was recruiting in my hometown (Urumqi). Holiday Inn was located in the best building in town which was owned by the Tourism Bureau. I believe that it was the only international hospitality company at that time and I applied to work there. I started at the entry level - as a waiter. Over the following 12 years I worked for Intercontinental hotels (later IHG), growing and developing, step by step, in this industry.

Interviewer: What inspired you to develop a hospitality business? What led you from working for others to starting your own venture?

Interviewee: I am a highly motivated person, perhaps because I am persistent. I also follow my heart. I had come to a stage in my life when I wanted to challenge or even compete against myself. Being involved in the services industry has made me grow. I have always wanted to internationalise China's hotel brands.

Interviewer: What defining characteristics are needed by hospitality leaders? Is there anything special that one might not find in other industries?

Interviewee: Perhaps I can give one example of another sector. The high-tech industries need many young people and other individuals who have the idea of transcending the times. However, in hospitality industry, a different type of leadership is needed. It's like an inheritance within families where a second generation inherits and learns from the grandparents - from top to bottom. This applies to hotels within the world's top 500 companies. A notable example is Marriott, which I regard as a family management business. If we consider another sector China's Midea (famous for its air-conditioners), is managed by professional managers. The two companies are both famous enterprises. Given this, why did they adopt their distinguishing forms of leadership? One consists of professionals, whereas the other has been run by three generations. In the end, I believe that differences between the two industries are the main explanation. Midea products involve introducing new ideas and pipeline systems. Each phase requires different things. On the other hand, the hospitality and services sector is more like a family, which explains the different styles of leadership.

Interviewer: What's your leadership style?

Interviewee: As a person, I pay a lot of attention to detail, am careful and thoughtful. I am also forceful and persistent. Finally, I emphasize the pursuit of excellence. Perhaps because I started my career at a basic and front-line position, I pay extra attention to the details and to the importance of logical thinking and being systematic. When I worked as Manager of the Stewarding Department, I was responsible for controlling the inventory of materials, including the turnover of utensils. That was where I acquired my knowledge about forecasting budgets, management of stores, and purchasing – it was over 20 years ago! This background explains why I can think logically through the details and deal with little things effectively. This is my way of thinking and my standard of behavior.

Interviewer: How have you been able to make your own company stand out as a market leader in luxury brands?

Interviewee: First of all, I am very familiar with the China's market, having grown up in this market environment. I have worked for Intercontinental Hotel Group (IHG), Shangri-la, Accor Hotels, Banyan Tree and the OCT Group. My

20 years of experience have taught me how to understand the prevailing market conditions and to be able to evaluate the competition. Secondly, the development of China's economy and hospitality in the past years has made me realise that it is now the best time to establish our own international hotel brands. I am a hotelier and would like to use my family name as a brand to help more owners and add to the credibility of our industry.

Interviewer: Can you share something about your WEI brand? I know that it contains many Chinese elements and uses these for the management and marketing style of your products. Also, can you talk about why and how you developed this concept and had the notion for such products?

Interviewee: I read many books about companies such as Marriott, Hilton, and Kempinski which have used the family name of the founder as their brands. From my reading, I concluded that the "rules of the game" in hospitality industry on a global scale were totally formulated by foreigners. There were eight "elders" in total, including five from the USA (Marriott, Hilton, Starwood, Hyatt and Wyndham), one from France (Accor), one from the UK (IHG) and another from Germany (Kempinski). All of the prevailing hospitality rules have been dominated by such companies over the past century. The standard operating systems that they have established are based on Western culture. I knew from reading the history of ancient and modern Chinese culture that China led the world for over five hundred years even 3,000 years ago. Ancient Chinese in Tang and Song Dynasties knew how to enjoy luxury, art, design, culture, cuisine, and leisure. In Qing Dynasty, for example, Manhan Quanxi (Chinese feast) was hosted in the royal palace. So, in my opinion, China has a long tradition of culture and luxury service. We should re-build this service and culture while making adjustments to the need of the fast-changing modern society. China has a history of 5,000 years and can be regarded as a senior while the West seems to be a 'fast growing youngster'. The senior possesses more cultural experience. However, in our contemporary period, we need to present our long-standing culture to the young in a more dynamic and modern way that they can experience and appreciate. Above all, I think the service industry in China will go global and will play an leading role on a global scale.

For this reason, I used my last name (WEI) as our brand. I later formed a design using divinatory symbols: W is three vertical strokes, E is three horizontal strokes and I is one (III, 三 , I in Chinese characters. There is a profound explanation for this in the famous national literature on *I-Ching*. One of the best known is that one produces two, two produces three and three produces all. In my logo design, three vertical strokes stand for mortal beings, three horizontal strokes represent the person, heaven and earth, and the one vertical stroke is for the individual. The two sets of three strokes means for the family, "I" means for filial piety. I hold the view that there should be an emerging element drawn from Chinese culture which has been accumulating over thousands of years. These divinatory symbols can be interpreted from many perspectives, all of which have their own attractive stories, such as the 64 hexagrams in I-Ching. There are five elements within the 64 hexagrams, namely: metal, wood, water, fire and earth, which correspond to different locations, weathers and people. China has a rich history of thousands of years and I believe that we need to integrate these cultural elements. So I have chosen my family name to name the hotels with a different sense of eastern elegance for our commitment to quality service.

Meanwhile, our brand has integrated Zen, Tea and Medicine. These elements have run throughout Chinese history and brought the highest level of luxury. Medicine implies the utilization of traditional Chinese medicine to maintain our health. Our products are focused on the spiritual uplift instead of a large capital infusion. With respect to our service, we advocate the concept of filial piety. The moral integrity of the Chinese nation is respect for elders while loving the young. I utilise the notion of filial piety to educate the young generations in China about providing whole-hearted service to others. When opening new hotels, we invite the parents of our staff to the site. We are committed to serving our guests heartily. In the future, China will become the largest origin country of outbound tourists and there should be industry leaders to join the elite team to promote the changes in global hospitality industry.

Interviewer: In summary, you have developed your brand by incorporating traditional Chinese culture and elements. What have been the main challenges?

Interviewee: Trust and reliance are currently the first challenges. China has experienced too many changes over the past two centuries. From ancient times to the present, and particularly during the recent century, China has not had its own luxury brands. There has been a lack of confidence and a lack of positive recognition of innovation. People have become crazy about making quick money and about surviving. I am not surprised that people hardly believe it when I promote my brand. For this reason, I feel that the major challenges are trust and credibility. The character and nature of the younger generation is another challenge. The current education system is not helpful when training them about pursuing a career in the services industry. In the future, the hospitality industry in China will employ more people. However, we do not have in place a complete system of education and training to keep pace with the times. To summarize, one challenge is to win the trust from owners and investors and the other is to redesign a service system that meets the demands from markets in China and the world.

Interviewer: Who is your industry role model?

Interviewee: I admire JW Marriott Junior. I have read all of his books, and believe that he tries his best to keep pace with the times in the hospitality industry. He makes several points that touch me a lot, such as following your heart, working hard and having an entrepreneurial spirit. He insists on expanding the business to become the largest one throughout the world.

Interviewer: What is the hospitality industry in China in your view?

Interviewee: The hospitality industry is a little similar to the management system in a country and has its own characteristics. I think that the hotel industry is more like a mini United Nations. Every country has its own cultural characteristics and different demands for hotel service at budget, middle and high levels. So, I believe that hotel leadership is a universal concept. Hotels have a culture and heritage.

Interviewer: How important is Guanxi in the hotel industry context?

Interviewee: As far as I am concerned, Guanxi is really a positive word. Hoteliers from all over the world are like a big family and work together to get stronger. For example, you can look for a person in any corner of the globe and that means building up relationships with other hoteliers through networks. Such relationship is particularly positive.

Interviewer: What is the impact of globalization on hoteliers?

Interviewee: Globalization presents the hospitality and tourism industry with special challenges. Ideally, I feel that globalization should support our efforts. In a way the whole world is developing too fast. Our generation of elders know how we walked to the present from the past. For the future, we hope for a stable and steady transition. Whilst this is our desire, the young generation view our ideas as outdated. I believe that we need to consider how to design a smoother transition and handover.

Interviewer: As your company expands globally, do cultural factors play a part, notably any challenges as a result of the Belt and Road initiative?

Interviewee: I have opened two hotels in Georgia with another at the pre-opening stage. I have opened a hotel in Hookaido, Japan and four are on the way. I have opened one hotel in Dubai and am planning to open four or five hotels next year in Europe. To be honest and this is just my opinion, I do not feel any big challenges. I have worked for multinational companies for over 20 years. I observed that they have a hundred-year history and make use of European methods. Over the past 20 years, China has applied the best hardware, software, food, design and so on. The most advanced techniques can be realized to full advantage in China, and the world may share our experience. China has been the largest country of origin exporting tourists overseas and is becoming ever stronger. Thus, when I step beyond our national boundaries and expand overseas, I see this as an opportunity to share our experience of 30 years with the industry. We need to innovate and lead the trend, instead of holding on to conservative values and opinions.

Interviewer: What's your opinion on hotels in Hong Kong and Macao?

Interviewee: Hotels are in absolute demand across the mainland. Since each city is relatively large, hotels are a less important thing. Though there is a significant and strong demand for hotels, we need to improve the level of quality of service and of staff. Hong Kong is an international metropolis with higher-quality personnel. I think that the challenge is for their industry to adjust its marketing strategies. It is worth noting that though Hong Kong should adjust its marketing strategies carefully, it should do so in a timely fashion, consistent with changes in the market, or else revenues will be negatively affected. In the case of Macao, I am optimistic because its current products suit China's development status. In addition to casinos, Macao operators emphasize a family-oriented approach, with many attractions that can be enjoyed with families. Thus, I feel that Macao's future development is promising.

Interviewer: Can you talk about leadership transition in the hospitality and tourism industry?

Interviewee: We tend to regard those who were born in the 1960s and 70s as a common generation (aged 40~59 at the time of writing). These people are experienced and have been educated and trained by international companies or by state owned enterprises. However, they will retire in the near future. Actually, in the not-too-distant future, the main workforce in the hospitality industry will have been born in the 1980s and 90s. The generation coming after those born in the 1980s is around 40 years old, which is a good age to become core members within the hotel world since they have grown up and live in good conditions. However, it is my observation that this group lacks determination. They cannot claim to have more knowledge than those from the 1960s and 70s, and they do not have the big dreams of the very young. Thus, people born in the late 1980s and early 1990s are more likely to take the baton from our generation and to contribute to leading the hospitality industry to a higher level.

Interviewer: What kind of challenges will face the new generation of leaders?

Interviewee: The challenge for the new generation of leaders is the changing customer. The major customers are becoming those born in the 1990s babies and the so-called Millennials. There is no doubt that products, service and marketing strategies will need tobe changed accordingly. However, the hotel industry has its traditional aspects which will never change, such as the back-of- house, and operations. In these terms, I think a challenge will be to get down to learning and improving themselves.

Interviewer: What is your opinion on customer satisfaction?

Interviewee: I think that employee satisfaction is important. Satisfaction is different in different cities, and even changes over time. From my personal experience, seasoned staff can be satisfied with fine staff meals, bonuses, holidays and some gifts. But currently, young staff do not care about these things at all. Instead, they need a goal, and ask you to give them time to achieve it. They do not think a lot about money, their family financial conditions are better, and they drive to the office every day. What they need is a sense of achievement and a title that you can offer them. It is totally different from previous times and we should design a new standard.

Interviewer: What role did studying play in your career development?

Interviewee: One is an insistence on my own efforts, by which I mean my eagerness to acquire new knowledge. So, I can say that learning is essential. Another quality is courage. I dare to do what others are afraid to do. I think study solidified my thoughts, making me clear about what I had done over previous years and the things that I should do in the future. As a result of studying at PolyU (The Hong Kong Polytechnic University), my method of analyzing alternatives and approaching problems has been changed. I now treat issues more objectively and rationally than before.

Interviewer: What is the future for developing luxury hotels?

Interviewee: A high-end market exists, and its development in China will last for 20 to 30 years, especially in the accommodation sector. In my opinion, business boutique hotels will be the next development opportunity.

Leading a Premium Hospitality Brand to Global Success from a Hong Kong-base

Interviewee: Mr. Clement Kwok
Title: CEO, Hong Kong and Shanghai Hotel Group
Interviewer: Prof. Brian King

Interviewer: Given your background in financial accounting, what prompted you to enter the hospitality field?

Interviewee: For all of us, I feel that it does not matter whether our professional foundations and training are in accounting, finance, law, or consulting, providing that we have been well trained to deal with different situations and find solutions to difficult problems. However, the professional knowledge can also be used imperceptibly. Looking to my starting point, I would describe accounting as a more retrospective activity, in that you essentially examine the records of something that has already been undertaken by others. I wanted to progress from the retrospective to working more in the "real-time". This desire prompted me into banking. There you are making deals with other people real-time and are involved in negotiations as the deal is happening. I found this aspect stimulating and it provided me with a valuable learning opportunity.

Reliable record-keeping is essential in accounting. When I was working in a banking environment, I came to realise the absence of formal "rules" when doing business. Instead you must negotiate according to your stated objectives but in a fair way. Doing so was a great experience. Over the course of my long period as a banker, I became aware that my essential role was as an intermediary. Essentially you are making deals on behalf of other principals with a bit of risk-taking. You might be doing underwriting or taking a position on something or publishing a public document, with all of the associated responsibilities. Despite the duty of care, this is not the same as running your own business, over which you exercise responsibility. I thought that the latter would suit me, since I tend to like bigger picture thinking, covering a longer time-frame. Given that I am fairly conservative by nature, a deal-based existence was not necessarily ideal for me; it was a question of finding a better opportunity.

MTR (Mass Transit Railway Corporation Limited – MTRCL) was a superb opportunity and it was great to get experience in corporate management at a time when MTR was highly active in international capital markets. It was a welcome challenge to acquire experience as an issuer in diverse international capital markets and as a deal-maker. Perhaps more importantly, I learnt a lot from MTR's excellent company management practices. The Corporation is well managed with great processes, structures in place and a strong organization. MTR has always maintained a high standard of corporate governance and management. As a significant issuer and given its ownership by the Hong Kong SAR government, it was a logical step for me to acquire experience in corporate management. It is perhaps predictable that once you have spent time as a Chief Financial Officer (CFO), you want to be a Chief Executive Officer (CEO). To draw a musical analogy, you want to conduct the orchestra rather than play a single part. The opportunity to become a CEO arose because I knew the Kadoorie family and they felt comfortable with me. This was why I came into the hospitality business. It was not because I viewed hotels as my preferred industry; it was more a case of considering how I could contribute skills such as financial and corporate management to an industry which I considered and still regard as fascinating.

I would like to pursue the orchestra analogy. I have to conduct the orchestra and make each section play in tune. How do conductors bring out the best from the play-ers? You must understand how to make the most of their strengths and build the right relationships so that they improve their performance and understand excellence.

The analogy shows the need for a conductor, even though the effort is collaborative. Though I have never played in an orchestra, I assume that a poor conductor would not have a well co-ordinated orchestra. The musicians would be unhappy about their playing and would not produce a nice sound.

The conducting analogy has relevance for hospitality industry. Since I cannot myself play the violin or another instrument, nor cook a fine meal or choose vintage wines or decorate a room, I must rely on the advice of experts for such activities. Hospitality is more than business. Personal relationships are critical and for much of the time, emotional factors are the important considerations when interacting with guests. Predictably, guest interactions are ineffective if you cannot interact well with your own people. The hospitality industry relies heavily on the human touch and I am highly conscious that our success or failure depends not on what I say or do sitting in my corporate office, but on the everyday interactions between staff members and those whom they encounter. The conductor analogy is appropriate because each hotel staff member has a particular skill set. In a people-centered business, leaders and managers must work with this spectrum of skills. Whilst we may pride ourselves on providing good service, it is essential to have a thorough understanding of how far you should go to satisfy the service expectations of guests. In ultra-expensive hotels catering to developed Western markets, customers may be paying in excess of a $US1,000 a night for a deluxe room (considerably more for a suite). Some guests understandably expect a lot in return. They not only expect you to take care of all of their requests, but also would like you to anticipate what they might want and to provide this as a very special and memorable experience. Since guests are buying an experience rather than a room, this must be curated and assembled as an outcome of multiple inputs.

Interviewer: What leadership characteristics are particularly important in hospitality?

Interviewee: The fundamental qualities do not vary much across the different business sectors that I have experienced. Ultimately, all businesses need high performance and effectiveness. One possible distinction of the hospitality industry is that it tends to attract and employ those with a more artistic or emotional disposition. This is positive in that settings such as a hotel lobby or a special event should convey an inviting feeling and ambience. To create this, we requires courage and a capacity to think "outside the box". Prior to joining Peninsula, I was at MTR (Mass Transit Railway) and worked with many engineering and construction graduates. Here, you have greater flamboyance and free-spiritedness and there are fewer people who have been trained like professional accountants. I have brought process, structure and transparency to this organization. This has provided staff with a guiding framework that helps them understand their roles and functions. It is important to marry the more artistic aspects of the process with a predicable structure.

Interviewer: It has been observed that the pursuit of short-term financial results is driving the major hotel groups. How do you achieve the right balance for your organization?

Interviewee: From my perspective, we should not be too prescriptive about desired outcomes and how to achieve them and this prompts us to avoid excessive growth. Once you expand beyond a certain point, you need to introduce new compliance and regulation procedures to tidy the process. Though we do not necessarily achieve the perfect balance between customization and standardization on all occasions, we advocate and promote the right mindset and psychology amongst our team. They understand the desired product and experience and marry this with the achievement of financial results. Though we review performance regularly and have conversations about futare plam, we grant considerable autonomy to our general managers. We also view our hotel general managers as businesspeople in their own right.

I attach considerable importance to the collective process behind our organizational decision-making. I work closely with the group management board (GMB). It consists of nine people, who are the executive directors and the heads of important functions such as group human resources and ICT. I would describe my basic style as follows. When we are making decisions or seeking project approvals, the responsible parties will bring to the table a thoroughly prepared paper that addresses all relevant points. The initiative may have a focus on financial, legal and technological issues or on human resources and/or corporate social responsibility (CSR). All of those with responsibility for the issue will be involved. The relevant parties are invited to join the discussion, including non GMB members. There is a shared understanding that any relevant comments or questions should be raised during discussions. Though I will not always agree with everything, I will try to explain my reasoning if I take a different view. But ultimately, I need to be the decision-maker. However, this only occurs following involvement and participation from those to whom I have referred. The rule is that a decision is collective once it has been reached. So if something goes wrong, nobody will return six months later and say, "Well, actually, I never agreed to that, but I didn't say anything". The principle is that we are in this together. That is my basic decision-making style.

Another characteristic is that I am not good at keeping secrets and I prefer to provide good transparency to my colleagues. I have a monthly conference call with all of the general managers in the company. The general managers of our various operations and functions call in and are briefed about what is happening. The aim is to avoid surprises. Up to 40 people participate in the conference calls and share information about what is happening. These are the guiding principles for my operation.

Interviewer: Are there leadership or innovation initiatives across the group about which you feel particular pride?

Interviewee: Starting from the basics, I am proud of the quality and prime locations of our hotels, particularly where we have developed new properties which have had positive community impacts. Then, I am proud of initiatives we have taken in areas such as corporate social responsibility, guest room technology and digital transformation. We have our own in-house research team that has developed our own bespoke in-room technologies and electronics.

Interviewer: Would you talk about your leadership and operation of the business in Hong Kong?

Interviewee: I grew up in Hong Kong and went to school and university in England. My children went to school and university in the USA. It is well known that Hong Kong has always been a place that has welcomed many nationalities. Drawing from this internationalized culture, it is notable that many of those who come to work in Hong Kong remark that it is easy to settle. Prolonged international exposure has given Hong Kong people good experience in dealing with people from diverse places and cultures. They have also gained experience by traveling extensively. Educational backgrounds are also diverse. Originally, much was Western-based with a lot of Hong Kong people going to the USA or UK to pursue their education. This has been supplemented more recently by others who have been educated in Chinese mainland and elsewhere. The diversity is beneficial because it creates confidence that you can operate in many different places from a Hong Kong base and be assured of the necessary experience and sophistication. With a Hong Kong based team like mine, you would never ask yourself, "Would this person be able to go and have a meeting in France or wherever?" You assume that we possess the necessary savoir-faire. Hong Kong is an excellent place for such international cross-fertilization.

Interviewer: Does the peer group within the Hong Kong business community seem to provide a strong basis for shared professional values?

Interviewee: Yes, the large number of well trained and educated people is a strength of Hong Kong and I really hope that this continues. We have well-established practices across the law, accountancy, and banking.

Personally, I feel that we sometimes forget the strengths of Hong Kong. It is efficient and has hard-working people who have diverse skills and who are good at execution. We should not forget this. I generally encourage people to remember the positives when I am interviewed.

Interviewer: What was it like when you started your career?

Interviewee: I don't particularly think of an inspirational Steve Jobs type of person. Instead, I focus on someone who had an impact early in my career, when I was still an unqualified auditor at Price Waterhouse (PWC). This was only six months into my working life. I was sent on an audit and I was informed that the senior manager would come and review the old papers and completed work. As a recent graduate, I assumed that a senior manager was of great importance and I was standing to attention and calling him sir. I expected someone high-level, like the president of the country. In fact, he was a wonderful guy - friendly and personable. Importantly, he dug into the details of our work. I had thought that this person was so high level that he would consider only the big picture. I was both surprised and impressed. I had little understanding or insight at the time and had not really considered my expectations – I was young and starting out. I was struck by the fact that this senior guy would be interested enough to go through the detail, to dive deeply and pick things out. I learnt a lot from this lesson.

Interviewer: How has Globalization and the Rise of China shaped Hospitality Leadership?

Interviewee: I'll answer this question at a broad level. As humans, we all like the good things in life. Once we have discovered beautiful hotel suites and spas, we want them. This is almost regardless of our origins. It is unsurprising to me that our customer demographics have widened considerably as we have extended our global reach. This is something that we welcome, though it involves learning to deal with the needs and wants of people from different cultures and nationalities. Managing this process involves reaching out and marketing to different segments, managing their requirements and providing a good experience. It is not complicated. Noting that globalization is probably too generic a word, we know that these forces have unleashed issues that include security, ethnic conflicts and diplomatic issues between nations. This affects how we manage our business and adds an extra level of complexity. However, we cannot influence or control these issues.

Right now, some of our businesses are affected by political and trade issues. For us, once an investment is made, we are stuck with it for the long term and need to have the staying power to make it work. You ultimately hope that you have chosen the right location in the longer-term. Having committed, you must "stick to your guns" and manage the situation as best as you can. Fortunately, our company adopts a very long term view and has the staying power and the right mindset to deal with such uncertainties. Part of my job is to chart our course based on the bigger picture and on the longer-term. However, there are many challenges in the contemporary world.

Interviewer: What's the impact of generational and technological changes on human beings?

Interviewee: There is a common perception nowadays that a young person is completely different to an older one. Relating back to my earlier comment about people wanting luxury, I feel that humans do not change much as they age. We generally want a bright future and career, to do well and to be free and satisfied. However, things are changing. People have many more options than before and some previously attractive choices have lost their appeal. The demographics of job opportunities have changed, particularly what people want and will accept. Some new jobs in business offer the prospect of different working lifestyles. For instance, where my son works – I won't say where – he can wear casual clothes to work. The team works hard and is highly productive. As a highly intelligent, well-educated young person, my son prefers to work in such a place where you can dress casually, rather than in a hotel where a jacket and tie is required. Choices about desirable environments are changing and I feel that we must adapt where we can do things which improve the quality of people's lives. However, we cannot abandon our core service principles or substantially change our most profitable offerings.

Adaption is easier in some industries than in others. In the case of the services sector, you must be disciplined and maintain certain ways of doing things. We have thought a lot about this. I am particularly mindful that technology plays a role where enhanced communications facilitate people's lives. Equally, technologies are making many jobs obsolete and what people will do in future remains unclear. In the past, someone could drive a train and expect a job for life. We are mindful of such changes. However, as I mentioned before, the basic principles remain the same - developing people, their skills and capabilities, giving them interesting challenges, opportunities for career progression and, honestly, financial rewards to afford a decent life. Whilst these things remain unchanged, the environment and the tools are being transformed.

Interviewer: The point about technology is interesting – may I explore your approach in a bit more detail? I accompanied a group of hospitality finance and technology professionals around the Hong Kong Peninsula Hotel and saw the efforts to balance the service style with the technology.

Interviewee: We are adopting an evolutionary and not a revolutionary approach. We respect our heritage which gives us strength. In acknowledging and celebrating past achievements and maintaining consistent basic values, we also need to embrace how the world is changing.

Interviewer: The various crests which are evident in the company headquarters seem to evidence an organizational identity that wants to show its rich heritage?

Interviewee: If you look at my business card, you will see that we have retained the original crest. This indicates history and heritage. However, we have changed the design and colour of the card to create a more contemporary look. Whilst it still a fairly traditional looking card, hopefully you won't look at it and think, "this company was operating only in the past and not the present."

Interviewer: What's your view about "Guanxi" in Chinese hospitality leadership ?

Interviewee: I don't think that leadership style should be associated with a particular ethnicity. During my career, I have observed different leadership styles depending on the company background and culture. It is well known that Hong Kong has many family-owned companies that were established by people who put in the effort themselves and worked their way up. It's a "hands-on", family management style. At the other end of the spectrum, you have so-called Western companies where there is a clear separation between ownership and management with independent boards. These contexts produce different leadership tendencies. We mentioned earlier that some mainland companies have evolved from large-scale state-owned enterprises. This produces certain values and shared understandings. So, I feel that differences may arise from the type of organization. However, in considering individual leadership styles, I feel that those comes down to the person. Particular organizational types generate their own leadership and management practices.

Interviewer: What's the relationship between the government and Hong Kong business operations?

Interviewee: I recall visiting many Mainland Chinese companies during my banking days, and they would say, "Please tell us about your business and its future prospects". The response would be: "Please let me introduce you to this government official and you will understand." Government policymaking and regulation played a bigger part in China then and affected what companies could do. Obviously, the hotel business in Hong Kong is completely deregulated. However, when I worked for MTR, great attention was given to government policies on transport and property development. Though the hospitality industry in Hong Kong is pretty deregulated I often need to obtain permission through planning approvals when doing business overseas. Often this is more about approval processes than about government policies. In private enterprise, you do business on the basis of negotiating commercial deals for a piece of land that you want for purchase. Government policies do not affect me much, except in a generic sense. However, it is generally helpful when governments enact policies that stimulate economic and tourism growth.

Leadership in a Relationship Hospitality Environment

Interviewee: Ms. Sonia Cheng
Title: Chief Executive Officer of Rosewood Hotel Group
Interviewer: Dr. Catherine Cheung

Interviewer: What are the characteristics of effective leadership within your organization?

Interviewee: In the hospitality industry, leaders must focus on *people*. It is the nature of the service industries to be day-to-day people oriented businesses. Hospitality leaders spend most of their time dealing with people through activities such as building relationships with hotel customers and with outside clients, for example with suppliers, partners and designers. There is also the managing and training of internal customers such as team leaders and members. Hospitality leaders are often challenged by human resources issues and by how best to develop relationships with people. Challenges include how to train and retrain and to develop talent; how to make people work together in a team; how to ensure that they love working and have shared beliefs; how to structure the company and ensure working harmoniously and effectively.

As CEO, I am very focused on the vision and trajectory of the brand. I strive to foster meaningful relationships with everyone I work with and instill in them the confidence to connect on a similar level with their co-workers and our guests.

Interviewer: What is the relationship between leadership and organizational culture?

Interviewee: The strategies that a leader adopts greatly influence organizational culture and are crucial for success. The culture of a strong company is not confined to possessing and embracing a "belief". It involves a deeper and more proactive type of management. For example, it permeates from daily briefing discussions to the operational tasks that employees perform. There is a need to manage the company culture, extending to almost every aspect of what employees do for the company. Hence, the organization culture is one ".... in which our people are valued and can grow and shine with us." (Faik, 2017)

Interviewer: What is relationship leadership? Are relationship leaders successful in leading their followers? Who do you think has effectively practiced relationship leadership?

Interviewee: Relationship leaders show humility to others, regardless of their achievement of success. My grandfather and my father were successful leaders and have provided valuable role models. My grandfather—Mr. Cheng Yu Tung founded New World Development, one of Hong Kong's biggest property companies. Coming from a humble background, he worked diligently to build his empire, despite lacking the benefits of privilege. The large number of employees who have worked for the New World group over many decades have shown loyalty, faith in the enterprise and great respect for my grandfather leadership. Both my grandfather and my father— Mr. Cheng Kar Shun evidently exemplify humility within the company. As well as being approachable, they have inspired and motivated their employees to progress and move ahead steadily in a fast changing business environment.

Leaders must build partnerships with their team if they are to ensure constant organizational improvement. A team should be committed, have a sense of belonging and contributing to the company and believe in the opportunities for growth. The world is changing fast and Rosewood Hotel Group is constantly driven to evolve and develop. The CEO role is about constantly pushing the team with new, fresh and innovative ideas for management and for the company. Rosewood is engaged in a constant process of collecting guest feedback. The most valuable insights describe specific guest experiences, whether positive or negative. This feedback helps to guide the various hotels with improvements to their service and organization.

Interviewer: How should successful leaders think?

Interviewee: The decisions that are taken by top leaders generally arise from their insights and beliefs. A number of successful top leaders such as Steve Jobs of Apple, Bill Gates of Microsoft and Mark Zuckerberg of Facebook had personal insights into the development of products. They followed their intuition and foresight, identifying a market need and proceeding to invent something new and innovative. They experienced tough beginnings during the development stage and during this stage their decision-making process was not reliant on research or on facts. One would never leave behind conservative and traditional ways of thinking if every decision depended exclusively on research and on facts.

Interviewer: What are your motivations being the CEO of the company? What expectations do you have for future growth?

Interviewee: I am passionate about hotels, about the opportunity to create a brand, I am fond of new things, a new project, to build something that you believe in and that will work in the market. In brief, passion is actually a driver.I believe that the hospitality leader gains satisfaction by finding new ways to take brands to the next level. I was graduated, graduating from Harvard University with a major in Economics. The combination of a Western education and Asian national culture has helped me to understand both eastern and western cultures. I believe that this provides me with open-mindedness and forward thinking to drive the company forward.

I aim and expect to take Rosewood Hotel Group to a new level. My desire is that Rosewood will be a brand that everyone knows as the leader in the hospitality industry, everyone wants to work for Rosewood and (the Hotel Group) keep expanding. Behind Rosewood's ambitious global development and expansion plan,there is a visionary and approachable leadership that follows the philosophy of "Relationship Hospitality". In 2018, Rosewood announced a plan for growth and expansion with the proposed addition of 50 hotels globally over the forthcoming five years, a 70%

increase in their portfolio across the four distinct hotel brands (Rosentreter, 2018). Allocating the resources that are required for each property is the biggest challenge for me. As a leader, I must ensure the consistency of each property in terms of quality and business performance. This depends critically on hiring and retaining the right talent. Given that hotels require such large numbers of talented people to operate, I believes that this will be the biggest problem across the hospitality industry. It is essential to find and deploy the right talent to remain competitive within the industry. On this basis, the entire processes of managing human resource and of employer branding are critical for the company. Rosewood Hotel Group has a variety of programs to support the recruitment and selection processes. Employer branding programs extend to school visits, internships, mentorship programs and school career fairs. It is essential to inform all comers that they can grow and learn within the company and to motivate them to follow a career path within the company. It is important for them to understand and embrace the company vision and culture.

Interviewer: Are there any gender gap in leadership? What is your view on women in leadership?

Interviewee: I advocate the elimination of the label "women leaders". I believe that stereotypical views will be perpetuated if more people talk in this way. I think that gender differences are not a problem in leadership and gender is not a limitation for a skilful and capable leader. In my view, the primacy of confidence is important than gender.

I describe the hotel industry as a dynamic "people" business. It encompasses everything to do with culture, marketing, design, finance, operation and service. In my opinion, humility, visionary, inspiring, convince people and fair are the characteristice of popular leaders.

Leading Hospitality Education to New Heights

Interviewee: Prof. Kaye Chon
Title: Dean and Chair Professor, Walter Kwok Foundation
Professor in International Hospitality Management, School of Hotel
and Tourism Management, The Hong Kong Polytechnic University
Interviewer: Prof. Brian King

Interviewer: How you were drawn into a tourism and hospitality career, and what keeps you motivated as a leader in hospitality education?

Interviewee: The answer to the first question is easy because I always wanted to travel and see the world. I chose hospitality and tourism as my career because I thought of it as one of the few that would allow me to fulfill that desire. As for the second question, I think the opportunity to make a difference is the main reason and is my continuing motivation.

Interviewer: Has this motivation always been there or has it evolved over the course of your career?

Interviewee: In a number of respects, I would say that it has evolved. When I was an undergraduate student in the USA, there was a visiting professor from Korea (he retired about 10 or 15 years ago). He later made reference to meeting me in his memoir, during my time as a student. He wrote that during his visiting professorship in the USA, he had heard about a Korean student in the class. Having looked out for me, he was surprised to find that I was fairly newly arrived in the United States. Though only a junior student, I was already appointed as President of the student association. The professor commented that I had obvious leadership capabilities based on how I was leading the meeting that he attended. Maybe becoming a leader in our field has been a case of fulfilling this potential. Perhaps I had the aptitude from a young age and an awareness about the importance of actively developing my leadership skills.

Interviewer: Let's move to the hospitality and tourism education sector. There are many general leadership theories that have been applied to diverse fields such as the military, politics or business. And there are evidently some particular leadership qualities that apply in hospitality and tourism and in education. Do particular characteristics distinguish leadership in our field? Can you share any examples of good hospitality leadership in Asia or further afield?

Interviewee: Leaders in all fields should possess some common traits. One of these is having good or common sense, because a lot of things in life are simple. So, a leader must possess common sense. Unfortunately, a lot of people seem to lack this and it hampers their potential to be successful leaders. To me, common sense involves having empathy for others and sensitivity, including cultural awareness. Having communication skills goes beyond language proficiency and concerns how you deal with others—what one might describe as the how of communications. Leaders should be determined and occupational capable of making decisions. I regard these as some common characteristics of leadership. But what makes hospitality and tourism different? We are constantly dealing with many different stakeholders and this makes effective communications particularly important. For leaders in factory settings, the job may be primarily about communicating with employees. In hospitality, many parties feel that they have a stake in the operation and it is critical to be able to communicate with them. Furthermore, I feel that aesthetic skills are highly variable. Some describe this as grooming, whereas others use the expression "presentation skills". Displaying aesthetic skills involves a capacity to see things differently, for example in more detail. It's about distinguishing both the forest and the trees. For me, this aspect is more important in hospitality and tourism. Small things can make a huge difference for customers. However, it's also important for leaders to understand the bigger picture. I have come across some leaders who are very good at the big picture, though cannot see the small details. Others are skilled at observing the small details, but miss the big picture (they are sometimes described as micromanagers). Some of the important traits for hospitality leaders include sensitivity, multi-culturalism, internationalism, and aesthetic sense. Leaders should understand the micro and macro environments and be capable of assessing their impacts on business. They should be proactive and anticipate in a way that allows them to respond effectively.

Interviewer: You mentioned your leadership in education, as well as in hospitality. You have also outlined some distinguishing characteristics of hospitality leadership. What about leading in education?

Interviewee: Firstly, one should understand the business environment – it has its own set of rules. Political skills are also important - how to convey your message in an appropriate manner. It depends on both the audience and on the situation. Sensitivity is important. When I was working in the United States, people appreciated it when you were more direct. Whereas, in Asia, people are usually a lot less direct. You should be more direct about some things when expressing your views, whereas other matters require a more diplomatic approach. You want to avoid causing uneasy feelings amongst your superiors or others. Then there's sensitivity to individual feelings. Maybe it is more appropriate to have a private conversation about a contentious point after a meeting with the party of interest, rather than in front of others. No single rule applies universally and you must make a judgment. For me, that is sensitivity.

Interviewer: Would you view situational leadership as a core value?

Interviewee: Yes. However, you need a grander big picture vision and to be capable of managing situations without compromising this. You will not make any progress if you are only managing the situation without maintaining your core values. The latter approach is simply a case of trying to please everybody.

Interviewer: How has your leadership style been shaped by experience and has it remained consistent or has it evolved?

Interviewee: Thinking about leadership generally, I feel that the characteristics of tyranny have remained constant over time. Leadership styles reflect one's personality and personal history as constants. In my own case, I feel that I have learned to communicate more effectively over time and through trial and error. I have learned from the experience of making mistakes. You acquire a new set of skills by accumulating experience and by making mistakes. When confronted by a new situation, you base your response on an inventory of past experiences. You have previously learnt how you ought to respond in that new situation.

Interviewer: Is there a leader for whom you have particular admiration?

Interviewee: I will give an example of someone from whom I learnt a lot. I had a superior who was very sharp - I have described him as a benevolent dictator. He was benevolent in the sense that he was venerable and sympathetic and was always trying to understand and communicate. However, he was also very firm about what he wanted to be achieved, regardless of any objections. Invariably, he was ultimately proven to be correct. Even when being confronted by a lot of resistance towards an issue about which he had already made up his mind, he always consulted. I learnt the leadership trait of determination from him. The superior whom I mentioned was labelled as a dictator, because he would push things through, even though he was doing his best to be sympathetic. The staff in that organization communicated with each other and relied on assemblies to reach shared understandings. He was also an excellent communicator who could place items on a shelf and then persuade anyone to buy them. He was charismatic and a good salesman. His communication style also brought out his credibility – this quality always shone through. I learnt the art of communicating from him.

I had another leader who was very creative. He was able to think "outside the box" and to use his problem solving skills. Unfortunately, he ultimately failed in his life and career because he lacked personal and professional integrity. My lesson from this example is that though creativity is important, integrity should always guide your life, both personally and professionally. Though you should be as creative and innovative as possible, this should occur within boundaries. I cannot think of a single hero whom I have followed in every way – what he or she does. I have, however, noticed that every leader with whom I have been associated has both unique strengths and unique weaknesses. I just learn from whatever I feel is important from individuals.

Interviewer: Beyond the external business environment of Hong Kong, Macao and mainland China, you are operating in a highly globalized environment as the Dean of the School of Hotel and Tourism Management. Do you have observations about operating globally from your base in Hong Kong? Has the environment shaped your hospitality leadership?

Interviewee: Coming to Hong Kong exposed me to a new set of experiences. The political and economic environments differ greatly from what I had experienced previously and which was familiar. It was necessary to understand this new set of rules and to apply them in a way that allows you to operate. Though nearby, Mainland China is very different from Hong Kong. You have to understand the relationships and how to communicate with and relate to the people. I communicate differently in mainland China from in Hong Kong. I think that you need to be both flexible and situational.

Interviewer: There is a considerable academic literature about Guanxi in hospitality and tourism. Do you have any observations about this concept as it applies in hospitality?

Interviewee: Actually, the Guanxi concept is not confined to mainland China. It is present in most Asian countries, including in Korea. I have already stressed the importance of relationships for hospitality leadership, though it is my understanding that Guanxi runs a bit deeper in China. Some relationships are purely financial or economic in nature. However, one cannot ignore the relationship itself. Maybe in one's 20s, relationships will prevent us from getting things done. In Asian countries, such as in Thailand or in Korea and from what I learned in China particularly, it is important to build rapport, friendships and trust. After that, everything becomes easier.

Interviewer: You have advocated the "Asian paradigm" or next wave of Asian leadership. This question concerns the role of relationships in this Asian wave. Are the roles that they play similar to Europe or America? Do they resemble previous waves or have unique features?

Interviewee: Understanding and showing sensitivity towards your co-workers, subordinates and clients is an important leadership trait, especially in Asia. Some Western managers lack such sensitivity and consequently fail as leaders when they first arrive in Asia. The following is an example of sensitivity on the part of a Western hotel general manager (GM). He was a legendary industry figure and served as GM in the same hotel for over 20 years. The property that he operated was successful across all areas, including employee satisfaction, and revenue generation. Then, a new GM arrived and said, " we can increase efficiency by reducing the number of staff … ". In some respects he was right. As he proceeded to make various changes, some employees were appreciative, whereas others complained – they wanted the return of their former GM. So, the new leader quickly failed and the company had to bring the former GM back to stabilize things. The role was subsequently handed over to another manager and the previous GM was installed as a Senior Vice President, overseeing the new GM. This is a classic example of sensitivity to how employees feel and cannot be simply explained by bookkeeping or financial returns.

Interviewer: I would now like to ask about globalization and the region. Hong Kong is now looking at the opportunities across the Greater Bay Area. What is your perspective about how this changing environment is impacting on leadership in our sector?

Interviewee: Though I may not be fully qualified to answer this question, I observe that Chinese companies are expanding rapidly overseas. Many are now experiencing turbulence because they are unfamiliar with understanding different (non-Chinese) markets.

Interviewer: Hong Kong is Asia-Pacific headquarters for many top hospitality companies as well as a global city. Is further progress towards globalization a positive for hospitality industry?

Interviewee: Globalization is generally a positive and something that we should embrace, though hospitality companies are adopting somewhat different approaches and strategies. Consider the examples of the Peninsula and Shangri-La hotel groups. Though there has been no official statement to this effect, the Peninsula group is undoubtedly globalizing. The company happens to be Hong Kong-based and is seeking to offer the finest possible hospitality services wherever they have properties. That's how they operate. Though Shangri-La are similar in many ways, they want to be seen as an Asian brand with Asian hospitality at their core as a value. Their model states that they provide Asian hospitality from a caring family. So, they want to be seen as Asian, just as the Bangkok-based Dusit International group wants to be seen as providing Thai hospitality. There are different ways of promoting this principle at a macro or country level. When Japanese firms are expanding, they want to be seen as Japanese firms. Whoever is representing Toyota in Thailand would be a Japanese person and customers would initially expect to encounter Japanese people working in the company. However, Korean companies have adopted a different approach. Some have policies that state, for example, that a local (ie Thai) CEO should be appointed to guide their Thailand operations. However, the company appoints this person behind the scenes - they rarely make public appearances or accept speaking engagements. These are different approaches and it has been interesting to observe the challenges being faced by such models, noting for example Toyota's overseas expansion.

Interviewer: Can you mention any challenges faced by leaders across the region? And what lies ahead for the following generation of leaders including current University hospitality students?

Interviewee: The future is bright for Asians and Chinese. Asian firms are expanding overseas faster than their western counterparts. We have a pool of talents who can become true global leaders. The linguistic challenge should be an areas of focus for future leaders. English has become the lingua franca of the business world. So, Chinese or Asian people who aspire to global leadership must be truly fluent in English. I think that is a challenge for our students; if they want to develop themselves as global leaders, they need linguistic fluency. If you look at some of the most successful Asian leaders, they have all been competent in English. So that is one challenge.

Besides, you have to be globally and internationally minded. Remember, for example, Ms Suphajee Suthumpun, the Group CEO of Dusit International recently addressed our commencing students. When she relocated to an executive role in New York for her employer (IBM), it was unusual for a female Thai to take up an executive role overseas in somewhere like New York. However, she was highly competent and was unafraid of the challenge. Many Asians are afraid and some even have what approaches a victim mentality.

Khun Chanin, Chairman of the Board, Dusit International talked to our students about the internationalization of Dusit. The company sent many Thai employees and leaders to Africa and the Middle East to work in their properties. Many wanted to return quickly to Thailand because they were more comfortable in their own cultural setting.

Khun Chanin has been fearless and he and the family have opened the door to a possible new life for their employees. However Thais, generally, seem to be very content and seek a happy environment. Given this, why bother seeking out new challenges? Khun Chanin explained that many Thais enjoy eating pork. However, when Thais travel to some Muslims countries , pork is not readily available. That sort of thing is a challenge for globalization.

The willingness of prospective hospitality leaders to be mobile is also a challenge for us here in Hong Kong. If you look at our hospitality student profile, about 73% are female. This is commonplace across hotel schools in Asia and perhaps globally. Though there are impacts on both genders, there are some additional complexities confronting women who wish to start families. Perhaps because of family and social pressures, it has been more challenging for them to leave their home environment and to advance their hotel careers quickly. As a consequence, many of our students prefer working in sales and marketing or in human resources, namely more stable roles which involve computer work and office operations. However, a limitation with HR for example is that any company has only a single Vice-President.

Interviewer: As a large number of highly qualified people enter the hospitality workforce, is this going to require a shift of thinking by the industry?

Interviewee: I think linguistic competence goes hand-in-hand with other skills. Consider the issue of attitude. Good language skills should be accompanied by confidence. If I have a deficiency in English and you don't understand me, confidence may prompt me to see this as a challenge for you, rather than as my problem. A sense of confidence can help to compensate for some limitations.

Interviewer: Does the next generation of leaders face challenges beyond language? I am referring to digital disruptions changing the industry structure and greater expectations about energy conservation. Such issues may require different thinking. Maybe our previous crop of leaders have not had to deal with such issues?

Interviewee: For me, the biggest challenge is the new generation itself, the group born in the 1980s and 1990s. The new cohort in Asia have been so well looked after that they are content and lack hunger. That is a big challenge when we compare this with the situation confronting previous generations, who wanted to prove themselves and who pursued their careers more aggressively. The new generation is pampered. In Hong Kong, for example, when I am returning from the gym in the morning, I often see that a child is walking to school, listening to music on his or her smartphone and there is a maid carrying his or her backpack. Sometimes, the maid is smaller than the student, but still carrying the backpack. I feel that this is symbolic. The new generations are so well looked after that I don't know what they can do by themselves. I mean, if the child is six or seven years old, I can understand, but with teens, why does the maid have to carry the backpack? I suppose they don't know how to make their own beds at home either, so what would they be able to do as leaders? I worry about that.

Interviewer: You encourage a sense of independence and responsibility amongst our students in the School and have shared your story about the value of learning to engage in manual tasks such as cutting carrots when you attended hospitality school. You also encourage the students in Hong Kong to wash the dishes as part of learning about the essential functions of a hospitality operation.

Interviewee: In Hong Kong, students don't wash dishes at home so they have the attitude, why bother to do it at school? I don't think there are any hotel schools in Europe or America that hire staff to wash dishes for the students. This is generational thing, a cultural thing.

Interviewer: Do you have any observations about younger leaders coming up and how the industry prepares to deal with the new generation?

Interviewee: I think that we need mentorship, whether it is through a formal or informal program. This is an effective way of grooming future generations. Every leader has to play that role of mentoring the next generation and of helping them to prepare for future challenges of leadership. In SHTM, we have a mentorship scheme for our more junior academic staff by more senior professors and another scheme which places students under the guidance of industry mentors.

Interviewer: Is the industry generally progressing well in this respect?

Interviewee: I sense some variation amongst across those who are involved in coaching individual leaders or organizations. Sometimes, the assigned coaches are too busy with their day-to-day operations and focus exclusively on meeting their monthly or even their daily targets. Good practice also involves building an informal grooming process and an evolving culture that develops leaders and leadership. We are doing this actively in the School.

Interviewer: In considering the achievements of the School of Hotel and Tourism Management at The Hong Kong Polytechnic University, can you share any closing remarks about your own leadership and of this School?

Interviewee: My leadership style and philosophy has been influenced by my religious orientation and by the concept of leadership that is present through the *Bible*. There are 66 books in the New Testament. If you collapse all of the words that are found in the Bible into one, that word is "love". The idea is that God loves his people and sent his own son to sacrifice himself to save them. So, the basic essence of the *Bible* is love. That is the source of my personal values. Second, we are all shaped by the culture within which we grew up. Since I spent my youth in Korea, my communication style has obviously been influenced by Korean culture. Then my understanding of the Western world has been shaped by living in the USA during my higher education and into my working life. I feel that this combination has contributed to my work in Hong Kong, which is partly Western and partly Asian.

My leadership style has been important for developing our School to where we are today. On the one hand, I always share credit with my colleagues. Such colleagues always play a role in creating a vision, however small. On the other hand, I then cheer on their vision with everyone else, so that they will be motivated to follow through. Everybody is a player, even if it is just as a cheerleader. The leader alone cannot do anything and cheerleaders help create a vision. I recall that when I came here, I single-handedly came up with the School motto. The motto was about leading Asia in hospitality and tourism. At first, there was widespread ridicule and sarcasm and people asked how I could legitimately claim that this school was leading Asia. However, some years later, people have started saying that I am right. one person said that we should make an even more forceful statement - that we are leading not only in education, but also the hospitality and tourism field. Now, we have introduced new practices and are an icon. I believe that if you have a vision and the capacity to communicate and to cheer everyone on, your colleagues and co-workers will buy into it. I view this is an important part of leadership.

The Innovative Perspectives of a Rising Female Leader

Interviewee: Ms. Winnie Chiu, JP
Title: President & Executive Director of Dorsett Hospitality International
Interviewer: Prof. Brian King

Interviewee: Hospitality industry has always spoken to me in a very personal way. As part of my family's business is owning and operating hotels, I've been fortunate to have been exposed to the industry from an early age. My first internship at the Ritz-Carlton Hong Kong over 20 years ago in particular really stands out. At the time, they were one of the most innovative high-end hospitality brands and each employee worldwide was given the Ritz-Carlton Credo – "We are Ladies and Gentlemen serving Ladies and Gentlemen" – along with Three Steps of Service and 12 Service Values to keep in their pocket. These included simple yet important service standards and core values which were instilled in their staff, including using the guest's name and always working to anticipate the needs of each guest. This is testament to how important a personalised, human touch is to a hotel brand's success and it still holds true today. The hospitality sector might be constantly evolving, but today's biggest consumer trends are globalisation and a higher and more sophisticated demand for customisation.

Interviewer: Did your family encourage you to undertake a hospitality internship?

Interviewee: I am blessed to have parents who always support me on whatever I choose to pursue. I did many internships, including one in engineering and spent periods working in both banking and retail. I soon realised that the most important thing to me is being able to provide a platform where people from all walks of life can grow and advance if they work hard. The 'barriers to entry' for the service industry is low – you don't necessarily need a higher education to excel or develop a career – and this really spoke to me. By creating a company culture where my employees are inspired, empowered and nurtured, I'm naturally instilling the same sensitivity and care when it comes to the service they offer our guests.

Interviewer: What motivates you to keep achieving in the field of hotels?

Interviewee: There is always something new in hospitality industry, whether this is opening up different geographic locations or extending the types of product on offer. Since the ultimate aim is to address consumer needs, we must stay in touch with their preferences. We (Dorsett Hospitality International) are owners as well as operators and this gives us the opportunity to add value to a property even if the real estate or property market is challenging at the time. We're very strategic in where we choose to buy properties, making sure that we not only buy at good value but that there is enough growth potential in the tourism for that area. I like to think of each of our hotels as an ambassador for the city in which they are located and this keeps it exciting. Our Dorsett Hotels' brand promise "Stay Vibrant" reflects how they've embraced the community and surrounding neighbourhood in each of their 27 cities, offering unique local experiences across art, culture and lifestyle to our guests whenever they stay with us.

Interviewer: What do you think of hotel services?

Interviewee: Hotel services includes much more than just hotels. What it all comes down to is service and you can only do that with the best people – those who are passionate about seeing your guests walk out with an even bigger smile than when they checked in. This is something that all leaders and managers should cultivate from within, which will then organically be reflected in how they treat guests. However, service on its own is no longer enough. Consumers not only want the best value, but an experience which speaks to and engages with them personally. As a hospitality leader you need to stay in touch with these nuances and make use of the different channels available to you.

Our newly-revamped website, for example, automatically customizes each visitor's experience best on their geo-location. Sensitive to the fact that visitors in China use different platforms, our website replaces Google Maps with Open Street Maps and shows China-friendly channels, such as WeChat, instead of Instagram or Facebook. We were also one of the first hotel groups to open a WeChat payment channel.

In the past, it might have been a luxury to provide the latest television model in every guest room – now it's considered part of a basic hotel service alongside a good bed and shower. The same can be said of coffee-making facilities, fast Wi-Fi and USB ports. Everything is always changing fast and this includes guests' expectations of the basic requirements when it comes to a hotel's physical accommodation. We were one of the first to offer a free phone with data in each guestroom so our guests can always stay connected. Now we've opened up food delivery to guests by partnering with Foodpanda to offer a seamless way to order from the best food spots straight to your room. Without leadership who is open and ahead of this change, it would be hard to keep up.

Furthermore, we're also planning to introduce 'Dorsett Discoveries' – a way in which to enrich our guests' experiences with carefully-curated happenings and partnerships that introduce where to 'eat, play and love' in each of the hotel's cities. We will be working with Affordable Art Fair and Sony World Photography Awards to go beyond the usual four-star experience and connect our guests with the latest in art and culture across our hotels internationally whilst attracting those who are passionate about art and their local city to our hotels.

I feel that I've truly cultivated an open and collaborative leadership environment, allowing our management team to learn from each other and our employees no matter their position or title. We recently finished a global branding exercise with all of our Dorsett Hotels local property teams, which allowed different departments to come together and brainstorm new initiatives and marketing ideas that they feel represent our brand and where we want to be. This not only gives our team deeper involvement and more ownership over initiatives, but it was also a great tool to gain feedback and learn from our employees who are on the front line servicing our guests every day. This type of inclusiveness as well as a willingness and enjoyment of customer service, dedication and the ability to think ahead is what I look for in leaders on my team.

Interviewer: Who are your hospitality leadership role models?

Interviewee: There are so many good role models out there, I wouldn't be able to identify a single individual since everyone is good at different things. That being said, I've been really impressed with how quickly Marriott has been able to pull all of its new resources together, following their acquisition with Starwood, to offer their guests with not only a wider variety of hotel offerings but innovative technological enhancements such as mobile and keyless check in through their app and live chats with your hotel host up to 24 hours before you arrive. Their asset-light model has allowed them to expand rapidly by attracting new owners to their various brands and to invest more in innovative sales and marketing. Also, Rosewood which focus on design and innovation, is distinguished by its approach to creating strong, modern and differentiated brands. They believe that true hospitality springs from the nurturing and building of strong and lasting relationships with fellow associates, guests, partners and the communities.

I do believe that Dorsett Hospitality International's vertically-integrated model allows us a more holistic and sustainable approach to scaling up our footprint. It also gives us the flexibility to optimize pricing and revenue in each of our markets, adapt and personalize our offerings more quickly and for better quality control when it comes to not only our products but service. By working with Strategic Partners such as Agora Hospitality Group and TransWorld Hotels, who have a collection of hotels in Japan and Europe respectively, we've also been able to make use of collective resources and use this expertise to continue to expand in new regions. Like Marriott Bonvoy, our recently-launched membership programme Dorsett – Your Rewards allows our guests to collect points and redeem benefits across our different brands.

However, we go a step further by offering a 'part-cash, part-points' model, which allows member to redeem rewards any time they wish, no matter how many points they've amassed.

Interviewer: Considering the wider business environment within which Dorsett operates, how does the fact that you are based in Hong Kong impact on your industry leadership?

Interviewee: Hong Kong is highly competitive within this wider business environment. The realities of the high cost of Hong Kong real estate alone makes running, let alone owning, a hotel expensive. This has forced us to be more disciplined when examining the price per square foot – something we monitor in all markets on a regular basis. Of course, as a hotelier, I am also concerned about service but we must also be practical and realistic. If a property is better designed as an office building, it may generate a better commercial return. This is where owning our own assets has definitely given us an advantage.

Due to the highly-competitive business environment overall, Hong Kongers tend to be very efficient. Even with a relatively lower staff-to-room ratio in Hong Kong, this has not made any compromise on service. Though we have met challenges over the last two years (due to a dip in tourism in Hong Kong between 2015 and 2017), we still outperform the market with an occupancy rate at around 86%~90% and recently our business has been doing very well with an occupancy at around 90%~95%.

The business environment is unique to every region. In Japan, for example, the style is more hierarchical and the importance and costs spent on food and beverage is a lot more extensive with lower GOP margins.

Interviewer: What do you think about "Guanxi" in business?

Interviewee: No matter if you're in Japan or UK, a lot of what gets done in business is all about "Guanxi" and the relationships that you've built and invested in over the years. As the world has become more global, everyone has connections nowadays. The difference is in being selective, respectful and genuine with those you choose to work and partner with and to make sure your business or brand philosophy has synergy and a shared purpose.

Interviewer: What's your business philosophy for operating across mainland China?

Interviewee: We focus our operations on the mainland Chinese market, though many of our properties are located outside China. We have a few hotels in China - in Shanghai, Wuhan, Chengdu, and in coastal cities. Since we have many Hong Kong properties, we focus for our strategy and operations on Chinese cities where there are parallels with Hong Kong. Because of our established experience of operating in Hong Kong, we were one of the first to get in touch with Chinese consumers when they started to travel outside the mainland. The first destination for such travelers would often be Hong Kong. This was definitely the case in the old days when they would definitely come here prior to venturing overseas. So we have a good understanding of their preferences.

For example, a WeChat payment facility is available in all of our hotels worldwide. We are also very Chinese-friendly from the time of the initial booking and reservation. We provide a full Chinese breakfast in all of our hotels worldwide, including in Europe. In our four-star hotels across Asia, including in China, we are familiar with the idea of providing a full range of amenities. However, I have found that four-star hotels in London won't necessarily provide all of these elements. This gives us an advantage to implement what we've learnt about our customers' behaviours and needs across all our properties and is something we will continue to do for our other demographics.

Interviewer: Thinking of your UK observations, can you elaborate about this different way of doing business – focusing on the China market and contracting out?

Interviewee: Technology is a huge thing for Chinese consumers and there is a proliferation of technologies and e-commerce platforms. The mainland of China is more advanced than Hong Kong in this respect, even more than everyone else across the world. We are now starting to work with an e-commerce platform where, if guests make purchases, they can pick it up at the hotel or can have it delivered to their room. Some items cannot be sent outside the mainland, so our Chinese guests can order from this e-commerce platform and then have the items sent to the mainland. The Chinese are also hungry for knowledge. As you are aware, some resorts offer something like a welcome drink. In the case of our brand we have a Dorsett wine hour, with free drinks for guests. It's not just a get-together – we introduce different topics of conversation. For example, one recent session was on contemporary art and some artists from Hong Kong art schools came to demonstrate and teach. The guests were hungry for knowledge. They also find it interesting when you highlight the heritage of the surrounding area.

Interviewer: What do you view as the major challenges for hospitality leaders across greater China?

Interviewee: I always think that finding talent is challenging – especially in second- and third-tier Chinese cities where hotel developments have sprung up quickly out of nowhere. Though they might have entered the city a bit too early, I feel that this will soon correct itself. There are also a lot more Chinese people working overseas who are starting to return on their own or through international groups, bringing with them more experience.

One of my most important principles for the group is our city focus, be it in Greater China or worldwide. This is because cities become progressively more important. People will continue to travel frequently to places such as Hong Kong, Tokyo, London and New York as they also act as hubs to nearby destinations. There are plenty of different opportunities even within the city category. As domestic travel is on the rise in the U.K., we are planning to look into offering a new serviced apartment category in London. My current focus currently is expanding in UK, Japan as well as entering Australia in the next few years.

Interviewer: What are some leadership challenges in hospitality for upcoming generations?

Interviewee: In considering the next generation, I think of my children, my nieces and nephews. They communicate differently online and through social media and this is important to them. The purpose of hotels could potentially become something very different in the future. Holiday Inns might have been popular 20 years ago, but the current trend has moved toward co-shared resources. Young people are quite open to the idea of shared rooms, platforms and working spaces. It's all about associating with a particular brand because it aligns with their own lifestyle or ideas. I recently visited a few five-star hotels in Amsterdam and many of the offerings were self-service. I can see why many millennials like the flexibility of ordering and paying in their own time. That's why we've integrated a curated menu in collaboration with Foodpanda in our guestrooms, so our guests have the same type of independence and flexibility.

Interviewer: In hotel schools like our own, about 70% of the students are women. In Hong Kong these students encounter a lot of older, male Westerners operating and managing hotels. What is the future the next generation studying hospitality industry, particularly young women? Do you think there are barriers in the industry?

Interviewee: According to Julia Campbell, the founder of Women in Hospitality, in 2017, the hospitality industry was composed of 55.5% of women yet the majority of managerial positions were still held by men. However, at Dorsett Hospitality International the majority of our leadership team and hotel management are made up of women. There's definitely a need for greater gender balance in hotels and I do feel that as a female CEO myself, I am more sensitive to the needs of not only my guests but my colleagues – both male and female. If a colleague tells me that she has to go to her son's school interview", I would be the first one to tell her to go. Even my male colleagues express these needs to me too. While equal representation in both leadership roles and in the workplace is incredibly important, I think it's also about creating an inclusive, accommodating and nurturing environment for your company. It's recognising the needs and balance that individuals need to grow.

I believe it comes down to the nature of my business and the culture we've cultivated. Looking at our properties, most of our general managers have come from sales and marketing backgrounds. A lot of other hotel general managers have come up from F&B backgrounds – and that can often mean more men. A strong focus of our business is in sales and marketing.

Interviewer: Are you surprised that relatively few of our graduates opt to remain in F&B over the longer term? I sense that they want industry leaders to be open minded about pathways to the top and that they don't necessarily want the traditional path in progressing to leadership roles.

Interviewee:I don't find it surprising at all. The way in which companies are hiring is changing – especially in hospitality. You don't necessarily have to have gone to hospitality school to be successful and by bringing together likeminded people from different backgrounds to work together, they each bring new ideas and learnings that can help keep the company moving forward. Identifying someone's passion and being able to align this with what they do at work means you'll get a lot more from them as you're satisfying both their interests and the company's. At the end of the day, hospitality is all about offering memorable experiences and making genuine, human connections – you can't do this without investing in the right people.

Hospitality Leadership across the Greater Bay Area and Beyond

Interviewee: Ms. Pansy Ho
Title: Group Executive Chairman and Managing Director of Shun Tak Holdings Limited
Interviewer: Prof. Brian King

Interviewer: What was your turning point to entering the hospitality industry?

Interviewee:I became involved because of a few coincidences. Initially, I was starting my own corporate communications and marketing business after being involved with the family business (Shun Tak Holdings). This is the flagship enterprise which my father established when he was operating various conglomerates in Macao, extending across hospitality, real estate, and logistics. Even during my own days in PR and corporate communications, we encountered hospitality industry and tourism clients.

About 20 years ago, somebody was needed to assist with a corporate marketing proposal during the development of Macao international Airport. My father said that there were no very qualified agencies in Macao, so attention shifted to securing a Hong Kong-based company. Having initially anticipated the engagement of one of the "big four" agencies, this changed because of a combination of budgetary considerations, and, more importantly, concerns that agencies lacked a true appreciation of the positioning of Macao during that period. There was a grand vision to build a substantial international airport in small Macao and someone was needed to appreciated the Hong Kong and Macao relationship.

During a casual family dinner conversation at home I said, "Well, give me that job - I would love to be involved." Subsequent to the success of my first foray into

Macao, I proceeded to work as an independent consultant to the airport company, rather than being appointed to an executive role. Then my father said, "Well, everybody thought you did a decent job." There was a greater understanding of requirements by this later stage and an appreciation that beyond providing a public transportation service, but there was scope for further service improvements. In addition to improving the collective destination image, there was a need for more market- and customer-driven operations. The prospect of additional services could potentially expand the network effect because they were building an airport, but lacked an understanding how they could compete with or complement Hong Kong International Airport. How could they attract carriers across China and Asia to consider using the airport? So, from a relatively small research and positioning exercise, they realized the need for more relevant expertise. Since my father's investment company was a major stakeholders and partner, he thought, "Well, maybe you should join the company instead of just being engaged as an independent service." So, that was the starting point from which I embarked on developments across a bigger sphere. I have now accumulated almost 30 years of experience across the tourism and hospitality field.

Having become involved with the airport, I proceeded to take up a Directorship with a Macao airline. Building upon such relationships, the Macao Government Tourism Office became involved and helped to shape the tourism dimensions of the city on the eve of its return to sovereignty. A range of marketing and repositioning activities were needed if Macao was to realize its potential in full. My father informed me about an understanding within Macao at that time. In those days, the Macao Government Tourism Office did not directly operate the various international representative offices – each was a sole responsibility and there were only the gaming concessions, which were operated by my father. A period of transition was needed with the various international representative offices being transferred back to the new SAR government under the newly established MGTO. I was assigned the duty of assisting the transitional phase over a period of almost two years. I operated with MGTO as a partner and worked closely through this transition with the previous MGTO director.

We worked together on transferring some of the outpost offices and engaged in an exercise of interviewing and in establishing some new ones. I learned a lot through this exercise and became directly involved with tourism and hospitality indutry – in marketing, operational planning, and strategic management. Coincidentally that was the beginning, though I always had the interest and conviction. I never viewed tourism and hospitality as being exclusively about business and about commercial gains and returns. From the outset, it was all about understanding why and how this activity is important, given Macao's heavy reliance on creating the tourism economy. The transition was obviously for Macao's future development.

Interviewer: Some mainland executives whom we have interviewed moved into tourism and hospitality indutry from other fields. How about your transition from communications to leadership of a large corporation?

Interviewee: At the beginning, it was mainly a case of developing vision and mission to ensure the fundamental infrastructure. This involved providing the various industry stakeholders with a clear future pathway.

When I subsequently became a stakeholder with a commercial stake, it became increasingly important for me to appreciate the role of the other stakeholders, because they would ultimately be using the infrastructure. Equally I understand some of the demands and requirements in my own capacity as an involved party. We need to ensure that this is not just an idea but also that it is implemented. We need to put good ideas into practice and make them profitable and commercially rewarding. Some of this transition involved me in planning and implementation. I was formally invited and then tasked as a kind of engineer to restructure the "beacon" co-business that operated a Hong Kong and Macao ferry operation. I was placed in charge of the whole operation and needed to start looking at the needs of our immediate operation as well as from the wider perspective of the tourism economy. How could we turn the business around and survive in a fact changing environment? I soon realized that it was a lot more complex than I had imagined. It was a case of going back to fundamental business principles, namely cost management and human resources, and evaluating future prospects. I orchestrated the re-engineering that proceeded.

A major merger and acquisition activity came next, involving a merging of our operations with those of some of our competitors. This produced a stronger team and ultimately led to the elimination of duplication and competition. Through that process, we undertook a serious evaluation of the supply and demand, and anticipated some external factors, including operational related. You can imagine the various cost related concerns. It always seemed to came back to the same issue - how to work with our suppliers and clients. We needed to undertake a comprehensive review of the whole business strategy. From this experience of business operations, I have seen the industry assets from both the buyer and the seller perspectives. It's not simply just about building something and then selling activities to potential buyers. You have to be there 24-hours a day, constantly in touch with both your customers and with the industry as a whole. An important takeaway for me is that hospitality and tourism is an industry that encompasses a diversity of aspects, with many unique features. You will never be successful if you just sit in an office making high-level decisions or looking at a balance sheet. We need to be present at all levels of the operation.

We initially encountered a variety of labor issues which resulted from the merging of two companies with their disparate organizational cultures. From early in the process staff were concerned about their job security and career prospects. Strikes broke out even before the contract had been signed. We had to address the various human resource issues almost immediately. I found that you must learn about all aspects of dealing with and running this particular sector or business. It is never just a case of doing a top job – you need to be ready to roll up our sleeves and get your hands dirty. You need to tackle all sorts of problems.

Interviewer: Are there particular leadership traits that you admire in others either in hospitality and tourism or beyond? Do you have a role model or example of good practice from close to home or globally?

Interviewee: From my experience of reaching out to peer and leaders in the field, there is always a common feature, especially in tourism and hospitality indutry. This is a lifelong career and I have seen the multiplicity of components because my Shun Tak Corporation business portfolio involves investments in other fields such as real estate and property development investments and development. We must cultivate and nurture a certain expertise when handling such areas. One of the real estate disciplines is the need to "move on" once a project has been built and then sold. This is irrespective of how proud you felt about the achievement.

You may build upon your local expertise and learnings, to extend your scope overseas. The initial development achievement is already past, whether it is an existing building or a portfolio which you continue to own. You must periodically revisit your original intentions and might then undertake an upgrade or carry out improvements. These activities allow you to focus back on that particular project. Tourism and hospitality is always "24/7". Even if you already own a portfolio of over 500 hotels, you can never stop thinking about being up-to-date with key trends. In order to meet current and evolving standards you need to engage in constant upgrading of your service quality. This is driven by your customers and not by you. Customer demands are constantly developing and evolving and you need to engage in continuous upgrading. You cannot just say, "Well, you know, these are older properties so I don't need to worry about them - my sole focus will be on new territories and initiatives."

Everything that you do should be consistent and tight. Unless you work this way, things will eventually become liabilities. The host of different leaders whom I have met always evaluate their own relevance to current market trends and practices. This provides tourism and hospitality industry people with a unique and innovative character. There is a lot of hype that surrounds innovation, as if it is itself something new. But it has always been there. Innovation must be constant and unrelenting in hospitality, or success will be unsustainable.

Interviewer: What is the impact of the Greater Bay Area on the hospitality industy?

Interviewee: The huge subject of the Greater Bay Area has caught everybody's attention since it became national policy. We now realize that it is imminent and will be implemented. All the infrastructure has already been laid out. In my case we have had good fortune and luck because we had various involvements in providing some of the critical public transportation. By pushing forward continuously and expanding to survive, we needed to understand and learn for ourselves how the relationship would develop amongst the Pearl River Delta cities and regions. We started almost 15 or 20 years ago, when we were working out for ourselves where the business should head.

We were the first to know about the possibilities of what ultimately became the Hong Kong Zhuhai Macao Bridge (HMZB). Fortunately, I participated in the earliest discussions, prior to government involvement. I assembled a committee which was initially championed by the private sector rather than the public sector. My father participated in the early forums, advocating and analyzing the feasibility of building the bridge.

I can still remember attending an early meeting. I was told, "Pansy, once the bridge is completed, your ferry business will be finished - out of business." I said, "That's why it's even more important for me to be here. I am not an enemy nor a spy. I just need to learn and, perhaps you will need me later to figure out exactly what you need to know, drawing from my data and from our experiences. You will need these things to conceive the bridge design." So, I had good fortune. Over the past 10 years, Shun Tak has covered more and more destinations and connections, not only between Hong Kong and Macao, but also across the Pearl River Delta. We were also at the forefront of learning about the other places, not just in terms of geography or travel distance. We started working with people based in these cities and, from there, we learnt about their future ideas and visions - what they wanted to become, and how they perceive their goals in the construction of the Pearl River

Delta - what we now call the Greater Bay Area.

Though the Greater Bay Area is relatively small as a territory, it is expansive in many ways. There remains a very limited understanding about differences and similarities, even though we all speak the same (Cantonese) dialect. Despite the considerable commonality of culture, there are few direct relationships, except between Hong Kong and Shenzhen, Macao and Zhuhai. If we are talking about assimilating everyone, there remains a considerable distance between the different mindsets. This extends to perceptions about strengths and weaknesses and who should do what. We realized early that the task will need a game plan backed with concrete measures. Now, thanks to the national government, there is a clear Greater Bay Area policy directive regarding infrastructural developments and the operation of the concept. I believe that the growth of the various participating cities will lead progressively to greater clarity about how each of us can find our own advantages and collaborate.

It would be impractical for each of us to confine ourselves to a few very specific things and to become highly specialized. Obviously, some places cannot now specialize into new areas because they have already had a long involvement in their own and well established economic development. Specialization cannot simply be brought about through design and we each need to work together comfortably. Inevitably, there will be areas of overlap. You cannot, for example, dictate that only Shenzhen can develop this great technology-based industry and, that consequentially, other areas cannot. Instead, there has to be scope for some competition, consistent with the ideas of open markets. In considering how to build on current strengths and to growth, how should we take advantage of what each place has already established? We should then capitalize on this and pull together our various resources. In the case of Macao, for instance, we aim to be competitive, even if this means competing with, for instance, Hong Kong.

Manpower is a current are of concern. Though employment in Macao is now at full capacity, there is a strong initiative to develop the MICE sector. We are all aware that Hong Kong is a long established leader across Asia in this domain. We now need to work together for growth and a population of 70 million will allow us to do so. Guangdong province where the Greater Bay Area sits, with its 100 million inhabitants, already accounts for a third of China's total economic capacity. There is considerable room for international enterprises to capitalize on this unique opportunity, with the Greater Bay Area as their base. Substantial MICE capacity has already been built in Hong Kong and Macao and increasingly in Zhuhai (Hengqin Island). Instead of just competing to grab existing markets, we should all work towards expanding the footprint. The commitment to an integrated region is an interesting challenge and more new collaborative avenues will emerge. I foresee the establishment of a network of Greater Bay Area MICE associations, bringing together all MICE related operators. Honest discussions will be needed involving the sharing of expertise and resources across the tourism sector. We have all been saying that we will be better off after the arrival of the bridge because all of the elements will be closer. Everybody who would like to go to Macao can stay in one of the many newer hotels. Equally we should encourage Hong Kong to continue to develop new hotel properties. In my opinion, why not?

Whenever I meet overseas business visitors, they share their decision-making about whether to expand into different parts of China. When I ask whether they have been to Macao, they typically say no, they haven't. I urge them to go and see for themselves. Though they sometimes worry that their businesses might not apply there, that's not the key point. They don't really know whether their businesses are applicable or relevant until they get to see not just Macao, but also Hengqin Island and the diversity of other parts of Guangdong province. We view Hong Kong business differently, because everybody already knows that this is the first point of arrival for newcomers. They will continue coming and will never abandon Hong Kong. As an example, it's like travelling to Italy. We will almost always want to have a Milan stopover – to go shopping or to visit art galleries. There are the important hub cities - the major urban centers. But you also want to cover other places and expand your understanding of the country as a whole. So, this is what we have been doing with the Greater Bay Area. There's Guangzhou and Hong Kong.

There are tourism areas, like Macao, and to a certain extent in future, there will be Hengqin. All of this prospective development involves helping visitors understand the meaning, capacity and prospects of the Greater Bay Area.

It's not just Hong Kong and Macao that are important. The country will continue to grow as a whole and that will continue to create more opportunities for us.

Interviewer: What do you think about the farsighted transformational leadership for the Greater Bay Area over the next 20 years?

Interviewee: In my own personal experience over the past 15 to 20 years, I have never stopped learning about our own country's policymaking and development and the government's vision of China's capabilities and self-assessment globally. I also appreciate the Government's relationship with other countries and the need for diplomacy. One could say, "Why are you becoming so political?" But this goes beyond politics - it is about having a global perspective and a vision. In the past, we need to appreciate it was easy for us in Hong Kong because everything seemed to be commercially driven. Why? Though we are now trying to capitalize on emerging opportunities we don't even understand ourselves and how to overcome some of the so-called differences that have been highlighted. What are we supposed to do when foreign operators or investors want to work alongside us? It may be important for us to offer encouragement in our capacity as leaders.

We should continue to capitalize on the special energy that is shown by Hong Kong and Macao people. We already have considerable knowledge and experience about collaborating with overseas entities and personnel. We should also become more knowledgeable about our own country so that we can become a bridge. We are also great at enterprise. When outsiders can access different parts of this area directly, it will open up faster – maybe with local and international developments paced similarly. Should we call taking the initiative a special capability? Maybe this is one of the various types of leadership.

Interviewer: You have talked about opportunities for overseas corporations in the Greater Bay Area. Most of our hospitality students at PolyU students speak Cantonese,

Putonghua, and English. In light of your comments about the next phase of development how do you feel that Chinese-speaking hospitality students can broaden their horizons by thinking beyond Hong Kong and Macao?

Interviewee: When the SAR government wanted to open up Macao 18 years ago, the Wynns and Venetians arrived. When opening up in this way, it was evident that you needed to attract the best in the sector, rather than confining the opportunities to those who were already prevalent in Asia, including, of course, my father's company. That's the point - after 50 years of operations, you want the world's best expertise to provide a different perspective. It's not that Macao companies weren't doing a good job. But you needed to attract attention to reach a different level. This is not a comparison or criticism or a suggestion that foreign ideas are better or superior. In the end, they may also need to adjust their operations. They have to understand that they are trying to build a different kind of market, which is the biggest in the world. Consider the Fosun organization as an instance. This company was not from an entertainment or tourism background and has gone through a typical investment process. They have bought over the rights to Cirque du Soleil in China and are going to build a comprehensive presence for this in Hangzhou, with a theme park, hotels, training, a school, and so on.

It's not as if we never had circus capabilities. I visited Cirque du Soleil some years ago because they said they were the largest provider of such shows in Las Vegas, where the MGM resort is still their exclusive partner. That's the reason that we have always maintained contact with them, exchanging ideas about the prospect of working together, whether in Macao or with Fosun. There was some discussion for this particular exercise about other parts of China. When I went to see them in Montreal, I discovered that 30% of the crew is Chinese. It is just that now they are returning to China and are bringing their creative ideas. They already have many years of experience and of exposure in other markets and they are going to bring that to China. Firstly this will provide a fresh perspective on our own Chinese performance, appreciating how they might transform their perceptions of this skill set for entertainment purposes. I can foresee that there will be future benefits for both sides. From now on we, will look at a new generation of partnerships and collaborations involving the co-development of new tourism and entertainment ideas. I sincerely believe that this will happen and that it could be very powerful. This is what innovation is about - putting good ideas together. It is no longer a case of just getting one party to adopt the ideas of another or of forcing each other to become half-equipped. The idea is to start an entirely new creative stream.

I believe this can happen and to an extent, it's what I'm doing in Macao through my partnership with MGM. When we created our properties, it was never going to be a "Las Vegas type of thing". From the outset we were each determined to contribute our understanding of the requirements of our own kind of industry. We then tried to create something totally new and exciting. Only through this approach can we continue to attract customers. You already have 120 million visitors going abroad annually. There is no reason for them to stay if you only offer them an experience that is available in Las Vegas. Why would they come to Macao for that when they can go to Las Vegas? In the future, I think that it's going to be very competitive to target the 1.4 billion people that make up our population. This is probably the best place in the world to test any sort of new hospitality and tourism market concept!

Interviewer: What is your personal leadership style?

Interviewee:I like to induct and help the people around me, encouraging them to work towards a single goal. Ultimately, it's not just what I say or think. I'd like people to know that I'm here to help and to give the knowledge that can be provided by my team. I share the insights that I have with others and the capabilities to which I have access. I do a lot of my own research and can tell people from personal experience that it ultimately comes down to the preparation work - the research. Though you can always listen to other people talk, they ultimately reach their conclusions based on their own views. You are aware that there are obviously great minds who can provide interesting perspectives. It is my sincere view though, that all these great minds do substantial preparations before they draw their conclusions!

Interviewer: So, would you say that you are seeking to empower the people around you?

Interviewee: That's true. I demand that everyone around the table does exactly the same amount of work. We share our different views. At times, I may be in a better position to offer a critique and to explain why an assessment may or may not be entirely accurate. Ultimately though, it's about how I can assist those with whom I work so that we can collectively develop the same understandings and conventions.

Towards a Hospitality and Entertainment "Super-industry"

Interviewee: Mr. Francis Lui Yiu Tung
Title: Vice Chairman of Galaxy Entertainment Group (GEG)
Interviewer: Prof. Brian King

Interviewer: What prompted you to join the hospitality and gaming sector?

Interviewee: My father epitomizes the Hong Kong success story. He came from China to Hong Kong because of World War II. He had no education and had to start everything afresh. By chance, he ran into some friends in the construction business (during the early 1950s and 1960s) at a time when Hong Kong was in need of a lot of construction to build its core capacity and that was how he became involved in the industry. He embraced the opportunities, and grew progressively bigger. That was how the family got involved, starting with things such as ready-mix concrete, pipes, cement and quarries. We saw that the city was prospering and moving from industrial construction towards real estate. We re-estimated the role of big business and diversify the business. There is now a more widespread appreciation that hospitality complements real estate and adds greater value to neighborhoods. This prompts you to consider the spillovers when you are undertaking integrated developments, adding up all of the various considerations. That was how we got involved in the hospitality business. We were presented with an opportunity during the opening up of the Macao casino and gaming industry licenses in 2002. This was more or less a typical Hong Kong success story, where you basically followed the market and the opportunities. That's how we turned from construction towards real estate and then from hospitality industry into the entertainment business.

Interviewer: Following the opening up of Macao and the remarkable development of Galaxy Entertainment Group, what has maintained your enthusiasm, interest and motivation?

Interviewee: We feel that we have the capacity to build a "super-industry" by combining entertainment, casinos and hospitality. I've never seen this being done before in Asia. If you look around, there was nowhere apart from Las Vegas. When I was studying in California, I was close enough to Las Vegas to see its evolution from a gambling-only industry town into more of a super-industry, encompassing conventions, retail, lifestyle, leisure, food and beverage (F&B) and dining experiences. We saw the evolution and felt that it could also happen in Asia. We believed in the possibility and went ahead. Fortunately, we secured one of the licenses. Then we saw the dream – and it is still the dream – of becoming one of the top entertainment companies in Asia. We feel that we have the opportunity and have targeted the right market to achieve success. That is what provided the original motivation. The venture has subsequently grown bigger and bigger and the future potential is huge with 1.4 billion people from China, and with Macao as the only place where gambling is allowed. We have observed the emerging market – for example, we were talking about a middle-class market of 40 million in 2014. The emerging middle class of China could be up to 600 million in 20 years and they are potential customers. In this context, we feel that we have the capacity to be a really substantial player.

Interviewer: What do you think is the vital for leadership?

Interviewee: I have not given much thought as to whether I have been driven by a single thing or if it's a case of passion. Certainly, you can do nothing without passion. I mean, you can have all the talent in the world, be the smartest person, or you can dream big. However, if you don't have the passion … I dare say you won't go far, because the experience is painful as well as enjoyable. You do not only have to motivate yourself, but also all of the people around you. Hopefully, when you have 22,000 people circled around you (GEG has over 22,000 employees), who have been influenced by your vision, they will move forward together in the same direction. This can also be challenging. I feel that you need lots of passion and to communicate well. You have to explain your vision in simple language, so that your team members will understand and execute things as well as you do yourself. Passion is the reason we think we are capable of achieving this over a short period.

Interviewer: I sense that you have a fascination and passion for food and beverage (F&B)? In hospitality schools such as at PolyU, we teach that chefs are creative and F&B people generally are passionate. Though your engineering background is very different, you evidently have the same enthusiasm.

Interviewee:I guess that it takes passion to achieve a good outcome, whether you're a restaurant owner or an engineer. I want to give 110% for every job that I do. You cannot be successful without having such drive. If you complete a job and see that you've achieved 80% of your vision, that's really not good enough. Most people can do 80%, but you want people who are going to go the "extra mile". That's the challenge.

Interviewer: Can you suggest some words that you would use to describe yourself or which others might use?

Interviewee: For those around you to feel that they can work with you, integrity and fairness are critical. You have to watch everybody to ensure that they work the way they should, and you cannot show favoritism. Ensuring fairness for everybody is essential for a leader. For me, it is important that they are rewarded, as long as they perform. I would emphasize communications. If you don't ensure that communication is happening continuously, you will be unable to achieve your objectives. You must have the patience to hear what others are saying. Communication is basically one-way with many bosses. When I say communication, I mean that you need the patience to sit with your team members around you, look in their eyes and listen to what they have to say to you.

Interviewer: Is there any leader whom you admire, either within or beyond our field?

Interviewee: Many successful businessmen and world leaders are inspirational.

But, if you ask me who has ultimately most influenced me, I must say my parents. As a very traditional Chinese, my father has always been disciplined and demanding. At the same time and in the context of a Chinese family, my mother has greatly influenced my life and is perhaps the unsung hero. I guess every young person feels rebellious when he is being told what to do. If discipline is informed by love, you can ultimately have empathy. Having accepted that everybody is different, we can still work towards a common goal. I think that my mother taught me this. I don't think I would be as successful as I am today if I had gone down another path.

Interviewer: Phases three and four of GEG in Macao are ambitious and fascinating. You also have land for development in Hengqin Island, Zhuhai and various interests elsewhere in Asia. How will the various developments beyond Macao are combined with mainland China?

Interviewee: Firstly, You have to be creative. If you are to achieve longer term sustainable success, it's essential to have own brand identity and competitive edge. You need to accept that our customers in Macao differ greatly from those elsewhere and place them at the centre. What are their needs? Do they drink beer like other guys do in the States or elsewhere? Do they eat the same food? Do they enjoy similar amenities? If the answer is no, then you have to provide a convenient and comfortable alternative. Part of our success in Macao is because the complex is user-friendly. Customers feel comfortable and at home when they enter Galaxy.

I still remember, almost 15 years ago, a lot of my compatriots said that this approach would be unsuccessful. You shouldn't have this and you shouldn't have that and the room has to be this big and you have to have lots of bars. I don't think that my customers need these things. Before I started to take care of GEG, I was tasked with developing the mainland Chinese business for the family. So, I spent a lot of time in Shanghai, Guangzhou, and Beijing. It seems to me that understanding our customers allows me to create the service and hardware that they prefer. We don't have the same size format as our Western counterparts. When consultants come over, they say that we need this and that for our customers. In response, we say,

"Look, our Asian building is a bit smaller, so we don't need the same size rooms." I mean, it could be smaller inside a room, but maybe they need more amenities, like a boiling water pot. I don't know how many times you go into a hotel room where you have this teapot sitting right in front of you, with these noodles. We were the first to do that in Macao. I was also the first to propose the idea that the casino should be bright. I still remember those days when you went to a casino and it was always in the basement. For me that suggested that I shouldn't go inside because it wouldn't make me happy. Then, once you go inside, you can't get out again because everything is so dark and convoluted. But if you go into a GEG casino, it's bright, so you feel good, you feel positive. I want people to be able to come out having enjoyed themselves. We use bright lights and skylights. And you can see natural light coming in. I still remember that it was once indoctrinated into me that there should be no sense of time and no clocks. Once you go inside, you should forget the time. We didn't do it that way. And you can see the new generation of properties is also starting to do that.

Interviewer: Will the concept continue apply as the company expands? How much adaption will be required for the company ethos, particularly moving into Japan and other potential jurisdictions?

Interviewee: The "World Class, Asian Heart" idea emerged when I was considering a motto for our property. We were saying that, if we want to do something and do it well, it should be five-star. It should be scalable, allowing you to dominate the market. At the same time, we have a vision for the level of service provision to our guests. We looked throughout the world – you and I have done this – you return with the impression that Asian customer service is always the most attentive and respectful. Though it (World Class, Asian Heart) was originally more of a property-based statement, the statement took on a life of its own and grew into our company culture. That's why it's not a surface-level motto when we make the statement "World Class, Asian Heart". It's more about the GEG company vision - whenever we do something, it should be world-class. The World Class, Asian Heart notion has expanded beyond customer service.

The all-encompassing Asian mentality is incorporated in the design of our hardware. I feel that we can show that we are still in Asia, especially for Chinese people. We are now the second largest economy in the world and China's middle class is growing fast. We are a proud nation and have a number of Fortune 500 companies. We want to have something about which we can say, "This is our heritage." Most Chinese people want something that is modern, contemporary and fashionable and is also backed by a story of Chinese heritage. That is why I think the Asian Heart idea is now starting to mean more. We are finally seeing the merits of being proud of our own national culture and heritage. This extends beyond our service and service staff and encompasses a whole operating mindset. The planning, design and interpretation involves more Chinese heritage. I think that we have done this successfully because, if you examine our property right now, you'll see a lot of Chinese or Asian DNA. When you walk through (our properties), you feel this is "top-notch" as well as fashionable and contemporary. You can see and feel the Chinese DNA when you look a bit deeper. For example, our phases one and two of Galaxy Macao are designed around the peacock - a lot of our design is based around the idea of the peacock. For us, this is a very Asian thing, because for Asian people, a peacock represents peace and wealth.

Interviewee: Considering the Greater Bay Area, we feel that Hong Kong is obviously a well-known city and that this applies increasingly to Macao with the opening of the casino industry. Now, with a potentially integrated destination, you have Shenzhen, which is growing fast. There are 70~80 million people living across the Greater Bay Area. With the benefits of technology to provide connections between the various cities, the future looks great. By being connected, they should resonate with one other and generate sufficient energy to drive forward.

Interviewee: You have this multiplier effect. Maybe 20 or 30 years ago, the Guangzhou and Dongguan area was the industrial hub for Hong Kong. The centre of gravity then somehow shifted to Shanghai and to the Eastern China Delta. Commerce and business have prospered in Shanghai over the past two decades. However, Guangzhou and the whole of Guangdong Province are rejuvenating and resurgent. Technologies are a basis for the new economy and are being widely applied. As long as we do it right over the coming 20 years, we will enjoy longer term competitiveness. I still recall when Beijing was a technological hub before Guangdong took over. There's now a powerful base with companies such as Tencent and Huawei. You have Hong Kong as a commercial centre, Shenzhen as the technological hub and Macao now focusing on entertainment. When you add them together, they will be really powerful and it's my feeling that they will take over from the San Francisco Bay and Tokyo Bay areas. I see many opportunities for Hong Kong people under "one country, two systems". They will be able to take advantage of this and do something big. I feel that we should coach and teach our next generation and students about how to take advantage of this opportunity. I just wish I were 40 years younger! Just as I recall so many opportunities in Hong Kong in the 1960s, 70s and 80s which helped us to achieve our present wealth—think about multiplying that GDP by many times across the Greater Bay Area. How do we take advantage of that? We should educate people so they are not afraid of the competition. As long as the younger generation embrace Chinese language and culture, they can understand and appreciate the differences between Hong Kong, Shenzhen and Macao better than we have done in the past. I see many opportunities for younger people to take bold steps in starting up businesses across the GBA.

Interviewer: Maybe I can share a finance, technology and tourism connection with you? Many of our senior students in Hangzhou are enrolled in PolyU's School of Hotel and Tourism Management in a partnership with Zhejiang University –100 doctoral and 130 masters hotel and tourism management students. Many leaders from Figgy (Alibaba) are studying masters and doctorates. Why? Because Alipay has been a technology and finance company and they want the knowledge to put those two areas together with tourism and hospitality in a smart way.

Interviewee: Artificial Intelligence (AI) can be a big help for our hospitality businesses, though I feel that we have only scratched the surface and still have limited insight. We are developing an understanding of how technology generally and AI in particular can improve our business. Hong Kong has always been a financing hub and the collective power of these three elements could be huge.

Interviewer: Do the challenges ahead for hospitality leaders differ from those which confronted previous generations? Any things that they should take more seriously than previous leaders?

Interviewee: Perhaps the biggest challenge for younger people is that they are not as hungry as we were. When we were born in the 1950s and 60s, Hong Kong was really at the bottom of the pile. At that time, we were basically on the way up and we were hungry and ready to grab any job opportunity when it appeared. To some extent, young people nowadays don't have the same passion or desire to excel. For me it's really about self-discipline and that's why I say that you must have passion.

My father and the family have been donating to different universities. He also set up the Lui Che-Woo Prize. In addition, we established the HKD 1.3billion GEG Foundation to help young people to do better in Macao and across China. We are grateful for the opportunities we had. Coming back to the original question, I think we have too much of a safety net. The other thing is that back then we were only competing amongst ourselves. There have been 30 years of exponential growth following the opening up of China and we are now competing with 1.4 billion Chinese people. I feel that our young people should understand that there are many younger people who are chasing us and who are hungry. So, we need to embrace it. We have the excellent education system and the excellent business system in Hong kong. I think our young people should embrace the challenge, learn their culture and language, and understand how to do business in China. That way, they will have many opportunities.

Interviewer: What is your leadership style?

Interviewee: I will briefly mention my leadership style. I show respect to all of my colleagues. You should reach out and do more because it's often not just about money. Though we must pay our team members market salary, feeling recognized is also important. Team members should feel that you care about them. That's very important for me. We want them to feel proud.

Thank you for the questions – they give me time to reflect and to think about how to do things better.

References

1   Cheng, S and Wong, A. (2015) Professionalism: A contemporary interpretation in hospitality industry context. International Journal of Hospitality Management 50: 122-133

2   Cheung, C, King, B.E.M. and Wong, A. (2018) What does the Industry need to know about Chinese Hospitality Leadership? Journal of China Tourism Research, 14 (2): 177-192

3   Chon. K.A. (2014) Leading the Way. The Story of SHTM and Hotel ICON Hong Kong Polytechnic University, Hong Kong

4   Chon, K. (2018) Hospitality in Asia: A New Paradigm. Routledge, Oxford

5   Harris, R.A., Jago, L. & King, B.E.M. (2005) Cases Studies in Tourism & Hospitality Marketing Pearson, Melbourne.

6   Jian, H. and Cheung (2013) What Types of Experiential Learning Activities Can Engage Hospitality Students in China? Journal of Hospitality and Tourism Education 24, 2/3:21-27

7   King, B.E.M. and Hyde, G. (1989) Tourism Marketing in Australia Hospitality Press, Melbourne

8   Pacific Asia Travel Association (2019) Asia Pacific Forecasts 2019-2023. PATA, Bangkok

9   Smith, R.A. and Siguaw, J. (2011) Strategic Hospitality Leadership: The Asian Initiative John Wiley, Singapore

10   Waryszak, R. & King, B.E.M (2001) An Investigation of Managerial Activity Preferences in the Hospitality & Service Sectors. International Journal of Contemporary Hospitality Management 13 (4): 197-203

项目策划：段向民

责任编辑：段向民　武洋

责任印制：孙颖慧

封面设计：武爱听

图书在版编目（CIP）数据

旅游酒店业引领者之高端视角 /（澳）金博蓝，张玉艳，黄志恩主编 . -- 北京 : 中国旅游出版社 , 2021.7

ISBN 978-7-5032-6669-0

Ⅰ . ①旅… Ⅱ . ①金… ②张… ③黄… Ⅲ . ①旅游饭店—研究—中国 Ⅳ . ① F719.3

中国版本图书馆 CIP 数据核字 (2021) 第 031919 号

书　　名：旅游酒店业引领者之高端视角

作　　者：（澳）金博蓝　张玉艳　黄志恩

出版发行：中国旅游出版社

（北京静安东里 6 号　邮编：100028 ）

http://www.cttp.net.cn　E-mail:cttp@mct.gov.cn

营销中心电话：010-57377108，010-57377109

读者服务部电话：010-57377151

排　　版：小武工作室

经　　销：全国各地新华书店

印　　刷：北京明恒达印务有限公司

版　　次：2021 年 7 月第 1 版　2021 年 7 月第 1 次印刷

开　　本：720 毫米 × 970 毫米　1/16

印　　张：9.75

字　　数：155 千

定　　价：59.80 元

ISBN　978-7-5032-6669-0